A CHIROPRACTOR'S

Treasury

OF

Health Secrets

A CHIROPRACTOR'S

Treasury

OF

Health Secrets

Samuel Homola, D. C.

Foreword by
PAUL-EMILE CHEVREFILS, M.D.

Parker Publishing Co., Inc.
West Nyack, N. Y.

LIBRARY OF CONGRESS
CATALOG CARD NUMBER: 76-93056

PRINTED IN THE UNITED STATES OF AMERICA
B & P—13-133157-4

For Mary, Jane, and Bill

with all the affection of a "big brother"

Other books by the author . . .

Bonesetting, Chiropractic, and Cultism
Backache: Home Treatment and Prevention
Muscle Training for Athletes

A Medical Doctor's Foreword

I found the reading of this book most interesting and practical. Every page of it contains health-building suggestions that are based on scientific principles.

The book contains many recommendations that physicians and nurses offer their patients daily. Summaries at the end of each chapter record briefly the helpful hints developed therein.

Chapter 2, for example, tells how to relax tense muscles. The author describes a "six-step drill for complete body relaxation," which can be very important to those of us who want to learn how to overcome nervous tension.

The value of good feet is strongly emphasized in Chapter 10. Overweight and hardening of the arteries, the two greatest dangers of our times, are discussed in Chapter 5. Both disorders push many individuals toward heart disease. Diet and natural foods, discussed in Chapter 12, are not nearly discussed enough in the different media of information.

A Chiropractor's Treasury of Health Secrets is a book you will be proud to place on your bookshelf for reliable information in daily health matters. I believe that many people will find useful guidance here and will benefit from the various programs outlined in the book.

As a practicing physician, I recommend *A Chiropractor's Treasury of Health Secrets* to anyone who wants to add years to his life.

Paul-Emile Chevrefils, M. D.

What This Book
Can Do for You

Health is not something that can be purchased. Contrary to the wishful thinking of persons who are constantly looking for a magic potion, there are no miracle medicines that can cancel out the effects of continued neglect and abuse of the body.

Good health is the product of natural, healthful living, and it can be best maintained by constant observation of the laws of nature.

There is more to being strong and healthy than just eating health foods and taking exercise, however. Every part of your body must receive special attention and care.

If you are stricken with acute pain or illness, you should, of course, see your doctor. But the use of self-help techniques in the care of certain ailments may be more effective than medication in providing relief from symptoms.

Just about everyone, at one time or another, will suffer from one or more of the common health problems discussed in this book. The symptoms of these ailments can nearly always be relieved with self-help techniques. Most of these ailments can be prevented if you use this self-help *before* the symptoms develop.

If you must work for a living, the guidance offered in this book will prove invaluable in keeping you in the ranks of wage earners. Such common ailments as backache, colds, arthritis, heart trouble, bad feet, headache, and nervous exhaustion, for example, can cut deeply into your earning power.

You can help yourself—and your doctor—in the care of a great variety of disorders as set out in this book. Self-help can be a satisfying challenge—and it can save you money.

All of the various programs described in this book have been found to be safe and effective. Anyone can use them without fear of pain or injury.

Every chapter outlines a complete self-help program for a specific ailment, along with instructions that reveal the secrets of healthful living. All of the chapters combine to provide you with a complete and balanced health-building program that will add more healthful years to your living.

Samuel Homola, D. C.

Acknowledgments

A special thanks to *Bibiana Neal* for preparing the line drawings, to *Elvis Surles* and *Bob Hargis* for supplying the photographs, and to *Jimmy and Betty Rowell* for being such willing and outstanding models.

Table of Contents

Femoral Hernia in the Female ● What Happens When Hernia Occurs? ● The Protection of a Lean Abdomen ● How Charlie B. Cured His Hernia ● Early Exercise Is Better Than Late Surgery ● Selecting the Exercises You Need ● Three Resistive Exercises to Prevent Hernia ● Two Special Exercises to Reduce a Hernia ● How to Breathe to Prevent Hernia ● How Hernia Can Occur Without Pain ● The Pain of Acute Hernia

Eat to Remain Physically Attractive ● The Warning of Poor Health ● The Seven Basic Food Groups ● Natural Foods Are Best ● Special Diets for Special Cases ● How to Get All Your Vitamins and Minerals ● Vitamin A for Your Eyes and Skin ● Vitamin B₁ for Steady Nerves ● Prevent Premature Aging with Vitamin B₂ ● Vitamin B₆ for Healthy Teeth ● Prevent Anemia with Vitamin B₁₂ ● Other B Vitamins ● All Together: B Complex ● Vitamin C for Quick Healing of Injuries ● Keep Your Bones Strong with Vitamin D ● Vitamin E for a Healthy Heart Muscle ● Vitamin K for Normal Clotting of Blood ● Vitamins Must Be Accompanied by Minerals ● Calcium for Bones, Teeth, Nerves, and Muscles ● Building Rich, Red Blood with Iron ● Iodine for Weight Control and Improved Thinking ● How to Get the Most Out of the Food You Eat ● Improper Cooking Is the Greatest Killer of Vitamins ● How to Save Water-Soluble Vitamins ● How to Save Fat-Soluble Vitamins ● Beware of Fried Foods ● What About Frozen Foods? ● Canned Foods: Your Third Choice ● Avoid Synthetic Foods

Your Heart Can't Do the Job Alone ● What Makes Your Blood Circulate? ● How Gravity Affects Your Blood Circulation ● How Exercise Helps Your Blood Circulate ● How Respiration Aids Circulation ● How to Improve Your Mind Power with a Slant Board ● How Overeating Deprives Your Brain of Blood ● How to Activate the "Blood Pumps" in Your Legs and Your Trunk ● Leg Pain Caused by Poor Circulation ● How to Stimulate Overall Body Circulation with Water ● Aiding Your Circulation with Massage ● Special Care for Varicose Veins ● How to Care for Hemorrhoids

1

Improve Your Health and Relieve Your Aches and Pains

It's difficult to stay healthy in this fast-moving, highly competitive world in which we live. The rush of getting to work on time, the pressure of getting a promotion, the strain of keeping up with the Joneses, the problem of "eating out," the poisons of polluted air, and many other hazards of civilization are constantly chipping away at our health. *Many of the luxuries of "good living" present hidden hazards that are more dangerous than the most potent germs.*

Heart disease, for example, is the Nation's No. 1 killer, and it is caused primarily by bad eating habits and lack of exercise. Overstimulation of the nervous system by hectic living, cigarette smoking, and drugs also heaps abuse on the heart. The common cold is responsible for more lost wages than any other ailment; it may be caused more by "lowered resistance" than by germs. There are, in fact, many diseases that occur because of the body's inability to fight them off or because of a breakdown in the body's machinery —all because of bad living habits. Back trouble is second only to heart trouble as a leading cause of chronic disability among persons who must work for a living. Most of this disability can be attributed to back injuries caused by weak muscles, bad working postures, and improper lifting techniques.

If you don't make a special effort to take care of yourself and to control your environment, you're almost sure to suffer from illness or aches and pains —from your head to your feet. And if you don't know how to use natural self-help techniques in relieving your symptoms and raising your resistance, you may suffer the fate of those chronically ill persons who spend fortunes on patent medicines and doctors' fees. Many of these people think that there is a pill for every ailment, and that they need only to see a doctor to get rid of their aches and pains. These people never regain their health, and many of them turn to excessive use of medication for temporary relief of symptoms.

UNRELIEVED NERVOUS TENSION CAN LEAD TO A VARIETY OF AILMENTS

Simple nervous tension, which we all suffer from most of our adult lives, is a good example of an ailment that must be relieved at its cause if it is to be handled successfully.

If you take a tranquilizing drug every time you get even slightly nervous, you might become an emotional cripple who cannot even face the stresses of everyday living without using medication as a crutch. Many people become addicted to "tranquilizers." Some of them suffer from side effects that are more troublesome than their tension.

Drugs are, of course, sometimes useful—and even necessary—in the treatment of certain types of illnesses for short periods of time, but they cannot and should not completely replace self-help techniques that are designed to prevent, as well as relieve, such recurring disorders as nervous tension.

Many people dismiss nervous tension as "not serious." The truth is, however, that "nerves" can cause a variety of ailments—from arthritis to stomach ulcers—that cannot be cured with medication.

A nervous person's complaints may be ignored until it's too late. Then, when illness develops, the patient begins a futile course of treatment that does little more than relieve the symptoms.

Chapter 2, "How to Overcome Nervous Tension," describes simple tension-relieving techniques that you can use at home or at work to relax your nerves. Once you learn how to *prevent* a build-up of tension, you'll contribute immeasurably to your general health. You'll also be able to prevent many of the "medically incurable" diseases that seem to afflict so many nervous persons.

HEADACHE CAN BE RELIEVED AT HOME

One of the most common manifestations of nervous tension is headache caused by prolonged contraction of the muscles on the back of the neck.

If circumstances arise that do not permit you to avoid a build-up of tension, and a headache occurs as a result, there are several effective home-treatment techniques that you can use safely at home to break the tension and relieve the symptoms. Simple traction on your neck, for example, applied by a friend or a partner, at home or on the job, will stretch the "knots" out of the muscles around your neck and shoulders. Heat and massage applied in a special way will relieve soreness and tenderness caused by unrelieved tension.

Everything you need to know to withdraw from the ranks of headache sufferers is outlined in Chapter 3, "How to Banish Recurring Headache."

YOU DON'T HAVE TO SUFFER FROM CONSTIPATION

Constipation is another common but easily preventable disorder that can reflect poor health and bad living habits. Most Americans suffer from constipation. You will, too, if you don't make a special effort to avoid this distressing condition.

Good living habits and proper diet will banish constipation just as surely as the sun sets each day. Chapter 4, "How to Rid Yourself of Constipation," will tell you what foods to eat, how to massage your colon, and how to take an enema, as well as many other facts about establishing regularity.

A ten-point program for eliminating the causes of constipation will enable you to rise above the laxative habit that has gripped the bowels of millions of careless and uninformed Americans.

PROLONG YOUR LIFE WITH CLEAN ARTERIES AND A STRONG HEART

Hardened arteries, a leading cause of heart disease, can also be controlled or prevented by making certain simple changes in your living habits and your diet. If you can learn to avoid foods containing saturated fat, for example, you can prevent a build-up of hard fat inside your arteries. Certain other foods actually contain ingredients that help *dissolve* fat that accumulates in the blood.

Once you understand the difference between "saturated" and "unsaturated" fat, you won't have any trouble at all selecting wholesome, natural foods that will keep your arteries young and flexible.

Chapter 5, "How to Prevent Overweight and Hardening of Your Arteries," will tell you what effect the various types of fat will have on your body. This complicated subject is discussed in simple, easy-to-understand language so that you can be well-informed about "polyunsaturates."

It's also important to strengthen your heart muscle. You can do this with special exercises that use the large muscles of your thighs. And with a little extra effort, you can improve your physical appearance by shaping up your skeletal muscles and burning off excess body fat. If you do the right exercises

Figure 1-1. Overweight, lack of exercise, and too much smoking are major causes of illness and aches and pains.

correctly, you can accomplish all this with a minimum amount of effort. See Figure 1-1 for the typical person who doesn't care about his physical condition.

Chapter 6, "How to Strengthen Your Heart for Better Health and a Longer Life," will explain what effect the various types of exercise have on your heart. It also describes new and revolutionary pulse rate tests that you can use to test the strength and efficiency of your heart action.

Everything you do, every effort you make to improve your health in any way, will benefit your body in a number of ways. Exercises designed to strengthen your heart, for example, will help relieve or prevent nervous tension, headache, and constipation, as well as hardening of the arteries.

All chronic ailments have a variety of causes which must be removed in a general health-building program. This is one reason why you should *read this book from cover to cover*, no matter what your complaint might be.

NEW FACTS ABOUT "INCURABLE" ARTHRITIS AND "INFECTIOUS" COLDS

Medical scientists now know that poor health and lowered resistance play a major role in the development of such common ailments as arthritis and colds. Chapters 7 and 8, "How to Cope with Arthritis Effectively and Painlessly" and "How to Strike Out the Common Cold," will tell you what to do to help your body fight off these irritating diseases. New facts suggest new treatments for quick relief of symptoms.

Special ways of applying heat with paraffin, mustard, or wet towels, for example, can provide soothing relief for sore and swollen arthritic joints. A simple exercise with a padded foot stool will prevent bending and distortion of an arthritic spine.

All these "health secrets" are yours for the reading. What you learn about arthritis will go a long way toward filling your treasure chest of health.

There's also a great deal that you can do about the "common cold." Did you know, for example, that cold germs in the nose can be killed by breathing mildly acid water vapor? This is one reason why the use of vinegar in folk medicine seems to be effective in the treatment of colds. And did you know that you can control activity of cold germs in the atmosphere of your home by controlling the relative humidity?

A special diet, rich in Vitamins A and C, is also important in maintaining your body's resistance against invasion by cold germs.

Once a cold infection begins, there is no overnight cure. Your body must muster its own defense in throwing out the invading germs. But if you'll follow the instructions in Chapter 8, you can *prevent* colds—or at least relieve your symptoms and shorten the course of the infection.

YOU CAN GET RID OF THAT NAGGING BACKACHE!

About one out of every three people now suffers from backache. Everyone, at one time or another, will come down with a backache or a back strain. So even if you don't have back trouble at the present time, the chances are that you will if you don't do all you can to prevent it *before* it happens.

Chapter 9, "How to Use Home Treatment to Cure Your Backache," clearly reveals how you can prevent back strain and relieve the symptoms of backache.

Simple self-help measures, ranging from heat and massage to posture instruction and correct lifting techniques, can save you time and money as well as relieve pain and disability. There are even a couple of exercises that you can do that will loosen your spine and adjust your vertebrae with no more effort than turning over in bed.

Special postural exercises that are designed to stretch your spine and relieve pressure on joints, discs, and nerves will maintain youthful strength, health and flexibility. When your spine benefits your whole body benefits.

Moist heat applied over the back in a certain way can ease back pain, relax spastic muscles, and stimulate the circulation of blood around and through the joints and nerves of your backbone.

When you finish reading Chapter 9, your treasure chest will be over half full. This chapter alone makes possession of this book worthwhile. As the author of the popular book, *Backache: Home Treatment & Prevention*, (Parker Publishing Co., W. Nyack, N. Y., 1967), I'm able to pass along a few polished nuggets and gems that have proven to be invaluable to backache sufferers.

MANY HEALTH TROUBLES STEM FROM THE FEET

Most people don't realize it, but foot and leg trouble can cause backache and a host of other symptoms in other parts of the body. In many of these cases, a simple change in foot posture will relieve the mechanical strain that transmits a disturbance all the way from the feet to the back of the neck. You'll learn in Chapter 10 "How to Improve Your Health with Foot and Leg Care" and how such common complaints as headache and muscle spasm can be triggered by tilted ankles and flat feet.

A new 4-step program that includes self-help foot manipulation will give you a "new" pair of feet. A hot and cold water treatment will flush your feet and legs with fresh oxygen-rich arterial blood—and this is especially important in the feet where gravity and other factors normally interfere with the circulation of blood.

What you learn in Chapter 10 will literally start you off on the right foot.

FRANK TALK ABOUT HERNIA

Although hernia is a common condition among both men and women, not many people know much about it because few people talk about it. If you already have a hernia, you can pick up a few suggestions on how to relieve your discomfort by reading Chapter 11, "How to Stop Needless Suffering from Hernia." You might even be able to reduce your hernia permanently by taking a couple of special abdominal exercises that will develop the muscles around the opening where the hernia has occurred.

Some people inherit a weakness that contributes to the development of hernia. You may have such a weakness without even knowing about it. But if you know how to breathe during exertion, you can *prevent* hernia most of the time. This is a very important health secret that no one can afford not to know.

Unfortunately, everyone is a candidate for hernia under the right conditions. Study Chapter 11 carefully, even if you are not now suffering from hernia. If you don't, you might allow the development of an abdominal hernia that won't make an appearance until after you've retired from work. Simple instructions on how to breathe while you're using your muscles or tying your shoe can save you from an abdominal "blowout" that might require surgical patching.

BASIC HEALTH-BUILDING RECOMMENDATIONS FOR EVERYONE

In practically every ailment you'll read about in this book, you'll find repeated reference to certain health-building recommendations that are essential in the prevention and cure of disease. Some of those mentioned most often are (1) proper eating habits, (2) improved circulation, and (3) correct breathing.

Special chapters have been devoted to each of these subjects. Each chapter contains valuable health secrets in a complete self-help program.

Your physical appearance as well as your general health, the attractiveness of your skin, hair, eyes, and nails, depends upon *total* body care. This means that you must observe *all* the rules of good health if you want to be healthy and look healthy. If you have bad skin, for example, you cannot correct the condition by taking Vitamin A if you ignore all the other needs of the skin.

EATING YOUR WAY TO HEALTH

What you eat every day and how you prepare it is extremely important. Doctors can often predict the development of certain diseases by observing a patient's eating habits. When disease does develop, a physician might have to prescribe high-powered food supplements along with medication. But in preventing disease and correcting deficiencies, it will be necessary to follow certain basic dietary recommendations in order to assure *complete* nutrition.

Chapter 12, "How to Eat for Youthful Health and Strength," offers practical, everyday guidance in selecting and preparing wholesome foods. You'll also learn how to supplement your diet with highly concentrated "miracle foods" that will supply commonly deficient food elements. A little yeast powder or bone meal, for example, stirred in a glass of honey-sweetened milk will give you a tasty beverage that's loaded with vitamins and minerals. Tea made from certain roots and herbs actually contains hormones that can boost waning sexual powers.

Eating for health can be a pleasure. With a little imagination and experimentation based on sound nutritional principles, eating can also be rewarding and exciting.

IMPROVING YOUR CIRCULATION

Regardless of what you eat and how well you live, you'll have to do all you can to help the circulation of blood if you want to make sure that every cell of your body is adequately nourished and cleansed. Your heart can't do the job alone.

Chapter 13, "How to Energize Your Mind and Body with an Improved Circulation of Blood," explains how you can use certain muscles in your body as "blood pumps" to flush your tissues with fresh blood.

There's also an amazingly effective posture exercise, in which you do nothing but lie down in a special position, that will bathe your brain with blood and reverse the interference that gravity places on the circulation of blood.

Special soaks and tonics to increase the flow of blood through the skin will make your body glow with the color of youth.

BREATHING FOR BETTER HEALTH

Everyone knows that deep breathing clears out the lungs and helps the body get rid of its waste products. But few people know how to breath correctly, and some even breathe too much.

Chapter 14, "How to Breathe New Life into Your Body," explains the difference between "thoracic breathing" and "abdominal breathing." It also describes special breathing exercises that will strengthen "breathing muscles" as well as cultivate efficient breathing techniques.

An extra-special breathing exercise with a plain paper bag can be used to relax your nerves and restore the chemical balance of your blood when tension and anxiety cause you to overbreathe. Many TV and movie personalities use this paper bag trick to ease their breathlessness and nervousness before making a public appearance.

Proper use of the muscles in your chest and abdomen during breathing will actually help your heart pump oxygen-deficient blood through your lungs. With a little practice, you can train your body to function with more efficiency than you ever thought possible.

...AND A LOT MORE

These are only a few of the health-building tips you'll find in this book. Every chapter is filled with practical and effective self-help techniques, along with case histories of persons who have already benefited by helping themselves in using these techniques.

All of the home-treatment programs outlined in the various chapters can be carried out without expensive equipment or medication. Many of the techniques will prove to be so convenient and rewarding that you'll want to make them a permanent part of your way of life.

Fortunately, little actual effort is required in healthful living. It's just a matter of living the right way rather than the wrong way. All you have to do is make a change in your way of life. You can actually use food, air, water, sleep, sunshine, and exercise as tonics for zestful living and to postpone the aging process.

As the title implies, *A Chiropractor's Treasury of Health Secrets* will prove to be a treasure for persons who want to improve their health and relieve their aches and pains the *natural* way. There is, in fact, no other way to build lasting health with maximum resistance against disease.

SUMMARY

1. This book, describing drugless and natural self-help techniques, will provide you with the key to lasting good health and freedom from aches and pains.

2. Each chapter outlines a specific program for a common ailment.

3. Everyone, at one time or another, will suffer from *all* of the ailments discussed in this book; that is, of course, if early and active measures aren't taken to prevent them.

4. You can use drugless techniques to *prevent* disease. So don't wait until you get sick to make use of the simple self-help techniques you'll find on every page of this book.

5. Everything you learn in every chapter of *A Chiropractor's Treasury of Health Secrets* can become a part of a new way of life for you and your family.

Overcome Nervous Tension

Few people can escape the grip of nervous tension. And when the responsibilities of raising a family and conducting a business are complicated by marital discord, family strife, or inadequate finances, the tension that results can cause nervous symptoms that can be as disturbing or incapacitating as true physical illness. If these symptoms persist unrelieved over a long period of time, they can lead to actual organic disease.

In other chapters of this book, you'll learn that nervous tension can contribute to the development of such common ailments as headache, constipation, hardened arteries, heart disease, backache, arthritis, and colds. Your "nerves" can also cause stomach ulcers, skin diseases, mental illness, and many other disorders. So one of the first things you should do in building better health is to quiet the nervous storm that bombards your body and its organs with destructive impulses.

There are many causes of nervous tension. Some are worse than others. The emotional agony of failure or inferiority, for example, is much more damaging than the stress of everyday living.

Whatever the cause of your tension might be, it must be eliminated for permanent relief of symptons—and this isn't always easy to do. There are, however, certain basic techniques that you can use to relieve your tension.

RELAXING YOUR NERVES THE NATURAL WAY

Fortunately, nervous tension itself is rarely caused by organic disease. The tension that most of us suffer from can be relieved with simple muscle-relaxing techniques.

Whenever you find it impossible to alter the conditions that lead to a build-up of tension, try to set aside "rest breaks" so that you can break your tension with the six-step muscle-relaxing drill outlined in this chapter.

Beware of Tranquilizers

Don't depend upon the use of sedatives or tranquilizing drugs to relieve nervous tension from day to day. Remember that drugs of any kind can have serious side effects when used regularly or habitually. Whenever you do develop a case of "nerves," you'll be better off if you'll use natural techniques rather than drugs to relax your mind as well as your muscles and your nerves.

Begin by Relaxing Your Muscles

Although there are many causes of nervous tension, all of them manifest themselves in muscular tension, especially in the muscles around the back of the head and neck (see "How to Banish Recurring Headache" in Chapter 3). This results in a "tension cycle" in which nervous tension causes muscular tension, which in turn causes more tension.

If you can learn how to relax completely and frequently during the day, you can relax your nerves by relaxing your muscles. In the process of doing this, you can temporarily erase the day's problems from your mind.

Relaxing Unused Muscles

Probably the most important thing to do in trying to prevent a build-up of nervous tension during the day is to *relax the muscles you aren't actually using*. Many nervous and tense persons sit around as rigid as a store dummy whenever they're under pressure. They sit with their muscles contracted without even realizing it. Few people are immune to such tension.

The last time I visited my dentist, I discovered that practically every muscle in my body would tense up while my teeth were being drilled. I had to make a special effort to relax, only to have the tension creep back almost unaware. I kept gripping the chair arms with my hands, pressing my feet against the foot support, pushing my head back against the head rest, and wrinkling my brow. Each time I discovered that my body was rigid with tension, I made another effort to relax my muscles.

Just imagine how fatiguing and nerve-wracking it would be to remain so tense day in and day out without relief. Many people actually do endure such tension. Some may even feel that they are relaxed, even when their muscles are tightly contracted. Most of these people suffer from all of the side effects of unrelieved tension. Whenever I meet one of these unfortunate persons, I recommend the same body-relaxing secrets you'll read about in the rest of this chapter.

CASE HISTORIES OF NERVOUS TENSION RELIEVED

A traveling salesman who suffered from stomach cramps whenever he had a bad day could relieve his discomfort with simple muscle-relaxing exercises. "Sometimes I even stop along the road to take my exercises," he said. "Once I fell asleep on top of a roadside picnic table and nearly got arrested for vagrancy."

A tension-harassed housewife with two small children used the same exercises to relieve the weakness and trembling whenever she was overtaken by fatigue and "nervous rigors."

"Whenever tension begins to build up," she said, "I feel light-headed and weak-kneed. And if I don't do something to relieve my tension, I start trembling and sweating. Sometimes I feel as if I'm going to lose control of myself and run out of the house screaming. When I get that bad, I call my neighbor over to watch my kids for me while I take time out to go through the exercises you gave me. They always help, and I come back refreshed after ten minutes or so."

In another case, a school teacher who suffered from colitis and headache could relieve her symptoms by going through the muscle-relaxing drill during recess, at lunch, and immediately following school.

A personnel manager in a garment factory had wall-to-wall carpet installed in his office so that he could lie down on the floor and do his exercises. "When I get too tense," he said, "my back and legs ache and my neck feels stiff. I lie down on the rug by my desk and do my exercises *before* I start getting a headache. Sometimes I even do the exercises when I don't feel tense just to make sure I *stay* relaxed. I don't believe I could make it through the day without these little breaks."

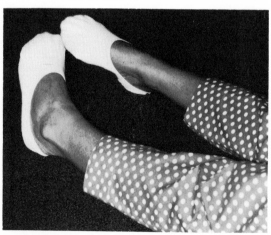

Figure 2-1. To relax the muscles of your legs, hold your toes together and then relax and let your feet flop apart.

DISTINGUISHING TENSE MUSCLES FROM RELAXED MUSCLES

In order to be successful in relieving nervous tension by relaxing your muscles, you'll have to be able to distinguish between a tense muscle and a relaxed muscle. In my practice of manipulating the joints of the spine, I have discovered that many tense persons do not know how to relax. Most of them cannot even tell whether a muscle is relaxed or tense. I have solved this problem with special exercises that first tense the muscles and then relax them while the joints move freely under the pull of gravity or in response to the pull of antagonistic muscles. Once you know what it feels like to relax, you should be able to relax at will.

TAKE TIME OUT TO RELAX

Whatever method of relaxation you use must require "time out" that will force you to slow down and relax two or three times in each hectic day. The time required to perform tension-relieving exercises is one of the secrets of their success. You cannot expect to relax if you "don't have time to relax."

The muscle-relaxing drill that I recommend to my patients has proven to be safe and effective, and it will work just as well for you. Go through the drill a couple of times each day or whenever you feel yourself getting tense. Take the phone off the hook and lock the front door so you won't be disturbed. Erase everything else from your mind. Concentrate only on the exercises you're doing so that you won't be bothered with unsolved problems.

Remember that if you can relax your muscles and *keep* them relaxed, you'll also relax your nerves, and you'll go a long way toward preventing many other disorders of the body.

A SIX-STEP PROGRAM FOR COMPLETE BODY RELAXATION

Lie on your back on a bed or rug so that you can relax completely. Begin with your feet and legs.

1. The Leg Roll

With your legs straight and flat and you heels about 12 inches apart, roll your feet toward each other so that your toes come together. Hold this position of tension for about three seconds. Then relax your legs suddenly and completely so that your feet will roll outward. Just let your feet flop back to a relaxed starting position. Lie still for a few seconds with your legs and feet as relaxed as possible. (See Figure 2-1.)

Repeat this exercise several times, each time striving for such complete relaxation that your feet roll back to the starting position without any interference from tense muscles.

IMPORTANT: Be sure to distinguish between the way your leg muscles feel while your toes are together and the way they feel while your feet are apart and relaxed. Whenever you're making any effort at all to hold your body in a certain position, your muscles are tense.

Let your feet and legs remain relaxed while you go on to the next exercise.

2. The Arm Drop

Remain lying on your back with your arms flat on the floor alongside your body. Lift your forearms up from the floor by bending only your elbows. With your elbows less than half flexed, hold this position of tension for about three seconds. Then let your arms fall back to the starting position. Relax completely so that your forearms will "drop like a rock." (See Figure 2-2.)

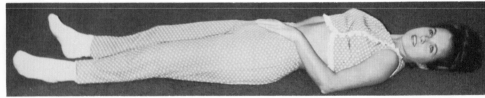

Figure 2-2. For complete arm relaxation, lift your arm up and then let it drop like a rock.

Repeat the exercise several times, each time striving for complete relaxation. Make sure that your hands remain open and relaxed.

Are your legs still relaxed? Both your arms and your legs should be relaxed when you begin the third exercise.

3. The Head Roll

Many people who suffer from nervous tension also have tense neck muscles. In order to make sure that your neck is relaxed along with the rest of your body, include this head-rolling exercise.

Turn your head as far to one side as you comfortably can and hold it in a position of tension for about three seconds. Then relax suddenly and let your head roll back to a neutral position. The pull of elastic neck muscles on the

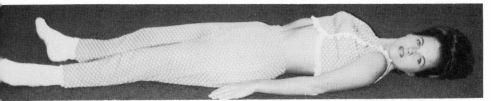

Figure 2-3. *Turn your head to one side as far as you can and then let it roll back to a neutral position.*

side opposite the contracting muscles will rotate your head back toward the starting position. (See Figure 2-3.)

Turn your head as far as you can to the opposite side. Hold it in that position for about three seconds and then let it spring back to a relaxed position.

Alternately rotate your head in each direction three times. Relax completely for about three seconds between turns.

Remember that this exercise, like all the rest, is performed while lying flat on your back. Do all six exercises before getting back on your feet.

4. The Wrinkled Brow

In many cases, a frowning, wrinkled brow is the only visible indication of tension. The brow is usually compressed into vertical furrows that have been created by movement of the eyebrows downward and toward each other. You can counteract contraction of these muscles by lifting your eyebrows upward to create horizontal furrows in your forehead.

Lift your eyebrows as high as you can. Hold them there for about three seconds and then let them fall into a relaxed position. Relax the muscles of your face so completely that you feel as if you're wearing a smooth face mask. You should literally erase the wrinkles on your face, and *there should be no vertical furrows between your eyebrows.* (See Figures 2-4, 2-5, 2-6.)

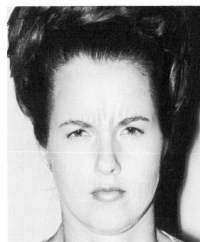

Figure 2-4. Vertical furrows between the eyebrows are a sure sign of tension.

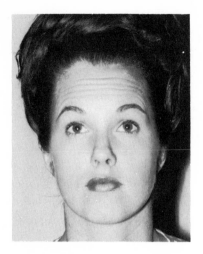

Figure 2-5. Lift your eyebrows as high as you can and then let them fall suddenly.

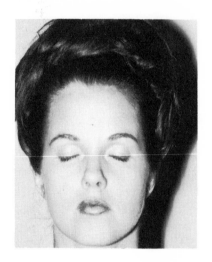

Figure 2-6. Erase tension wrinkles several times each day by letting the muscles of your face sag.

NOTE: Relaxing the muscles of the forehead and the scalp will permit a greater flow of blood to the hair roots for a thicker and healthier head of hair. Many chronically tense persons keep their scalp muscles so tight and contracted that blood can barely circulate between the skin and the skull. If your hair is thin, try to loosen your scalp by massaging it every day.

5. The Chest Lift

Breathe deeply through your nose, lifting your chest up high. Then let your chest collapse as the air escapes through your mouth. Do this three or four times and then lie quietly for several minutes. (See Figure 2-7.)

Filling and emptying your lungs repeatedly may make you slightly dizzy from hyperventilation (see Chapter 14), but this will aid in promoting relaxation.

As you lie completely relaxed, breathe naturally, without making any effort

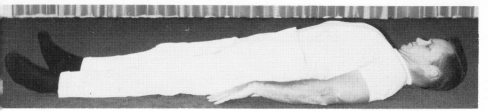

Figure 2-7. Lift your chest high with a deep breath and then let your rib cage "collapse" as you exhale.

to lift your chest. This should result in "abdominal breathing" in which there is more movement in the abdomen than in the chest.

6.   Double Check Your Tension

While you're lying relaxed, repeat each exercise once in order to make sure that your entire body is relaxed. Let each part sag as though it were lifeless. Pretend that you don't have any muscles and that you're unable to move. Imagine that you are a rag doll lying in a field of gently swaying flowers. Lie still for several minutes.

Go through the complete drill two or three times each day, or whenever you feel tension gripping your body.

Some people aren't able to relax because they aren't able to erase disturbing thoughts from their mind. If you can't create a mental blank during the rest periods, think about things you enjoy doing.

Remember that relaxation itself requires no effort. Don't try so hard to relax that you create tension rather than relieve it. Whenever you're resting, your muscles should be so relaxed that they do not exert any pull at all on your bones and joints.

A LITTLE EXERCISE MIGHT HELP

A small amount of exercise at the end of a particularly trying day is sometimes helpful in relieving nervous fatigue and tension. It's important, however, that you distinguish between physical fatigue and nervous fatigue before considering exercise. If you work hard all day and perform physical labor, you probably need to rest rather than exercise at the end of each day. But if your fatigue is the result of tense muscles and nerves produced by brain work and static postures, you can soothe your nerves and relieve your aches and pains with almost any kind of exercise.

Try to exercise just after work or a couple of hours before your evening meal. But don't overdo it. You should feel refreshed rather than fatigued when the exercise is completed. Select a form of exercise—such as swimming or bicycle riding—that you find convenient and entertaining.

RELAX IN A ROCKING CHAIR

As we grow older, most of us find that we can relax better in a rocking chair when we're just sitting around the house. One reason for this is that the light and rhythmical contraction of muscles in maintaining the rocking motion helps to keep the blood circulating. Alternate contraction and relaxation of the muscles also tends to relax muscles and nerves.

ADEQUATE SLEEP IS IMPORTANT

Regardless of whether your fatigue is nervous or physical in origin, you need a certain amount of sleep each night if your body, mind, and nerves are to recuperate fully from day to day.

If you're suffering from physical fatigue, you'll feel rested after getting adequate sleep. But if you're suffering from nervous fatigue, you may "wake up tired" each morning, regardless of the amount of sleep you get. You need the sleep, but you may also need to make a change in your way of life. A little regular exercise will sometimes jar the nervous system out of a rut.

YOUR NERVES NEED VITAMIN B AND CALCIUM

Nutritional scientists tell us that the diet of the average American is deficient in Vitamin B—and this is the vitamin that builds and nourishes the nervous system. One reason for this deficiency is that most of us satisfy our appetite with white bread and other wheat products that have been so highly refined that all the Vitamin B has been milled out.

Sugar Destroys Vitamin B

Excessive use of concentrated sugars and starches deprives the body of Vitamin B by "burning it up" in the body's metabolic processes. The more bread and sugar you eat, the more Vitamin B you lose and the more you need.

If you're nervous, overweight, and addicted to carbohydrate foods (sugar is a carbohydrate), you may need much more Vitamin B than you're getting in such an unbalanced diet.

If you use a lot of sweetening, use mineral-rich honey, unsulphured molasses, or brown sugar instead of refined white sugar. You'll feel better and you'll have more energy. It's important to remember, however, that your body manufactures the sugar it needs from the carbohydrate foods you eat. So the less sugar you eat the better.

Supplementing Your Diet

Few people today present obvious symptoms of vitamin deficiency, thanks to the addition of synthetic vitamins to milk, bread, cereal, and other popular food items. But if you don't eat whole wheat products, plenty of lean meat, and other natural foods, you may suffer from just enough Vitamin B deficiency to produce "subclinical symptoms" or vague and nonspecific nervous complaints that defy diagnosis or cure.

I recommend Vitamin B Complex to all my patients who suffer from "nervous trouble" and then advise them to make a special effort to eat foods that are rich in Vitamin B. Once the deficiency has been corrected with concentrated food supplements, adequate amounts of the various B vitamins can be obtained from a reasonably good diet. It's important to remember, however, that your body doesn't store Vitamin B as it does some of the other vitamins, so you should make a special effort to obtain adequate amounts each day.

Don't Forget Calcium

Calcium is also important for a strong and stable nervous system. In the diet of the average American, milk is the most important source of this mineral. Unfortunately, many adults do not drink milk. Be sure to study Chapter 12 for instructions in selecting and preparing the foods you need to build healthy nerves.

ADOPT A RELAXING HOBBY

Everyone, especially a nervous person, needs an entertaining hobby that will get his mind off his troubles. And whenever such a hobby provides a little physical exercise, so much the better. But don't be like the tension-packed businessman who took up golf and then slammed his club into the ground every time he failed to hit the ball properly, or the fisherman who becomes "sick" every time a "big one" gets away. Try to select a pastime that won't make you nervous or raise your blood pressure.

It's always a good idea to vent your temper and frustration in physical activity whenever social or business pressures push you to the breaking point. However, your recreational activities should never be so difficult or competitive that they add a sense of failure to your frustration. I know one executive who has a heavy punching bag hanging in his basement. When he comes home tense and irritable, he pounds the bag until he dissipates his excess nervous energy and his body relaxes from physical fatigue.

A chaplain I know prefers to lift barbells for bodybuilding purposes. An insurance salesman enjoys bird watching and a walk in the woods. An architect has a simple photographic darkroom where he develops and prints his own pictures. All these people find relief from their tensions in the pleasures of their pastimes, and they do so without taking on a challenge that may create anxiety or lead to failure.

GO EASY ON CIVIC PROJECTS

If you're suffering constantly from unrelieved nervous tension, you should probably avoid all unnecessary responsibilities. I've seen persons suffering from nervous fatigue (also called "neurasthenia") plunge headlong into a nervous breakdown because they didn't have the courage to say "no" when they were asked to assume responsibility for a "part-time" church or civic project.

It is, of course, a good idea for nervous persons to turn their attention to other matters in order to keep from thinking about their own troubles. But such diversion should not load them with take-home problems that cause them to worry or lie awake at night.

THE SEDATIVE EFFECT OF WARM WATER

Whenever you're nervous and keyed up because of emotional stress and strain, a warm tub bath will calm your nerves.

STIMULATING THE NERVES WITH COLD WATER

If you're frequently sleepy and drowsy from inactivity or oversleeping, you can wake your sleepy nerves by massaging your body with a coarse bath glove that has been dipped in ice water. Take a warm shower first and then gradually turn it down to cold before you rub your body with ice water.

This is a powerful form of stimulation that can fatigue the body if it's overdone. Just two or three strokes over each body part will be adequate. Dry your body immediately with a coarse bath towel.

SUMMARY

1. The most important thing to remember in avoiding unnecessary tension during the day is to relax the muscles you aren't actually using.

2. Make a special effort to relax *all* of your muscles a couple of times each

day by first tensing your muscles and then relaxing them so that you become as limp as a dish rag. Try the muscle-relaxing drill described in this chapter.

3. Remember that if you can relax your muscles and keep them relaxed, you'll also relax your nerves.

4. When the day's work is done, erase unpleasant thoughts from your mind by indulging in entertaining pastimes and thinking about things you enjoy doing.

5. If you don't perform physical labor all day, a little light exercise immediately after work will dissipate nervous and muscular tensions.

6. "Bad nerves" can cause a variety of illnesses. If you can learn to control your nerves, you can improve your health immeasurably.

7. For your nerves' sake, be sure to study Chapter 12 for food sources of Vitamin B and calcium.

8. If you sit around the house for long hours each day, you can probably relax better in a rocking chair than in a straight chair.

3

Banish Recurring Headache

If your daily routine includes the muscle-relaxing program described in Chapter 2, you may be able to prevent tension headache. But if your neck muscles do tighten up occasionally to cause headache, you can use the simple home-treatment techniques described in this chapter to relax these muscles and relieve the symptoms.

SELF-HELP CAN SAVE YOU MONEY

It has been estimated that Americans spend $300,000,000 a year on popular headache remedies, none of which do more than temporarily relieve the symptoms. Yet, seven out of ten adults take medication for headache at least once a month.

If you can learn to use self-help techniques that prevent as well as relieve symptoms, you won't have to rely upon expensive medication that may have side effects.

See your doctor first in order to make sure there's no organic basis for your headache. Then make an effort to help yourself, according to the instructions in this chapter.

TIGHT NECK MUSCLES AS A CAUSE OF HEADACHE

There are many causes of headache. However, 90 percent of all headaches are of the tension and migraine variety, with seven out of ten of these being triggered by simple tension. *The most common cause of "tension headache," for example, is prolonged contraction of the muscles on the back of the neck.* Persons who suffer from this type of headache will very often point out that the back of their neck is tight, sore, and stiff.

Little is known about how tight neck muscles actually cause a headache, but we do know that the pain usually stems from reflex dilatation (expansion) of the blood vessels around the brain. This causes a throbbing pain that pounds in rhythm with the heart beat.

Brain tissue itself is not sensitive to pain. But the walls of the blood vessels are richly supplied with sensitive pain fibers. When these vessels dilate enough to stretch the vessel walls, each beat of the heart transmits acute hammer-like pain to the head. The constant pull of tight neck and scalp muscles may also irritate nerves to cause a "dull" headache.

EFFECTIVE RELIEF FOR HEADACHE

Most tension headaches can be relieved with such simple home-treatment remedies as moist heat, cold packs, massage, and traction. Whenever possible, the treatment should be applied as soon as the first symptoms appear. If tension in the muscles of the neck should persist unrelieved, inflamed and spastic muscles may cause a deeply rooted chronic headache that won't respond immediately to any type of treatment. Prolonged contraction of the muscles may also jam the joints of the neck together and pull some of the bones out of alignment. Irritation of the nerve trunks between these bones may then cause agonizing neck, shoulder, and arm pain.

CASE HISTORIES OF TENSION HEADACHE HEALED

Martha B. had been suffering from headache and neck trouble for many years. She worked as a secretary during the day and then went home in the evenings to do housework for a husband and two teenage boys. Her headache always started in the afternoon when she began to get a little tired and then got worse when she started her housekeeping chores. Doctors had treated her with tranquilizers, hormones, antihistamine, and other dangerous and potentially habit-forming drugs. None did more than temporarily relieve her pain, and the soreness in her neck persisted. In addition to her nightly headache, she was beginning to experience a throbbing ache that radiated out into both shoulders and down her arms.

Expensive medical examinations failed to reveal a cause for Martha's headache. Some of the doctors, suspecting that she was "nervous" or emotionally disturbed, told her that she must learn to "live with" her condition. One doctor told her that she was simply working too hard. "I sure am," she said, "but there's nothing I can do about that until we get out of debt. There must be *something* that I can do to relieve my headache."

When she started the self-help program outlined in this chapter, she began to improve immediately. After several weeks, she suffered from ten-

sion headache only occasionally, and this could be relieved with simple traction on her neck.

In one case, a telephone operator who attributed her frequent headaches
to "the tyranny of a heartless supervisor" was able to help herself enough,
through steps described in the next section, to discontinue frequent trips to
her doctor for her headache condition.

A struggling businessman who had a cold, nagging wife found that nothing would "cure" his frequent headaches. He did find, however, that under
my suggestions he could relieve his symptoms each day by heating and stretching the muscles of his neck.

A draftsman who spent long hours drawing house plans found that he got
better results by putting an ice pack on the front of his neck.

If you suffer from recurring tension headache, chances are you can benefit from the same self-help techniques that others have used. You may also include these techniques in your daily routine as a matter of prevention. None
of them are potentially harmful, and they may be used in conjunction with any
type of treatment your doctor might prescribe.

FIVE SIMPLE STEPS IN PREVENTING AND
RELIEVING TENSION HEADACHE

Whenever you feel your neck muscles tighten up, or whenever you begin to have a tension headache, any one of the simple treatment methods
that follow may afford relief. If one doesn't work, try the next, and then use
any combination that seems to get the best results for you.

You should try to eliminate sources of tension that are aggravating enough
to give you a headache. When this isn't possible, you should make arrange-
ments to use traction or some self-help technique when tension begins to
build.

1. Stretching Out Tension with Traction

Whenever a muscle becomes tight from nervous tension, some of its muscle fibers actually contract. Since this is an involuntary contraction caused
by a nervous reflex, it can usually be relieved by placing pressure on the
muscle or by stretching its fibers.

There are three ways that you can apply traction to the muscles of your
neck. Pick the method that best suits your circumstances. Any kind of stretch
on the neck will realign its joints and relieve pressure on nerves.

Figure 3-1. Let your head fall back so that the base of your skull will rest against the top edge of your hands.

A. TRACTION WITH YOUR HANDS: Whenever you're alone, on a bus, or in some situation that does not permit use of either of the other two traction techniques, use this method of stretching your neck when tension begins to build.

Place both hands on the back of your neck with your fingertips overlapping. Then let your head fall back with your neck muscles completely relaxed. Your hands will act as a wedge to pry your neck vertebrae apart while the base of your skull is resting on the top edge of your hands. Drop your head back several times while pressing your hands against the back of your neck. Try to relax completely. Whenever possible, do this exercise while leaning back in a reclining chair so that gravity and the weight of your head will make the traction more effective. (See Figure 3-1.)

Then drop your head forward and stretch the muscles on the back of your neck by pressing the base of your skull forward and upward with your hands. (See Figure 3-2.)

BREAK YOUR TENSION BY MOVING AROUND: If you work over a desk, a typewriter, a sewing machine, or in any occupation in which you must keep your head tilted down for hours at a time, you'd be wise to straighten up and drop your head back several times each day—and for two good reasons.

When the neck muscles are forced to remain contracted for long periods of time in holding the head up over the chest, an accumulation of lactic acid and other waste products irritates the muscles to cause inflammation and spasm. There is also a danger of reversing the normal curve of the neck spine.

Figure 3-2. Stretch the back of your neck by pressing the base of your skull forward and upward.

41

Once this happens, the muscles of the neck must work even harder in holding the head up. All this can cause neck pain as well as headache.

Try to take time out to relieve the tension on your neck every time you feel a little fatigue building up in your neck muscles. When the day's work is done, vigorous exercise will sometimes prevent headache by dissipating nervous tension and relaxing tight muscles.

B.   TRACTION WITH A PARTNER: If you work alongside someone who is willing to lend a hand in stretching the muscles of your neck, you can get a heavier and more specific traction with the partner method. If done correctly, this technique can be applied safely and effectively.

Sit erect on the edge of a low stool or "side saddle" in a straight chair. Instruct your partner to stand behind you with the forepart of his right foot (his left foot if he is left handed) up on the edge of the chair seat. Then, with his hands cupped around the base of your skull and your jaws on each side, and his right elbow supported by his right knee, he can stretch your neck by raising the heel of the foot that's on the stool. His wrists should be held rigid so that movement of the supporting knee will lift your head. (See Figure 3-3.)

If you are a tall person, it may be necessary for your partner to place a book or two under his foot on the stool in order to get a couple of inches of traction.

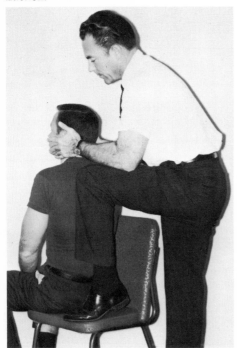

Figure 3-3. *Traction with a partner can be applied conveniently on the job or during a rest break.*

Instruct your partner to apply a slow, steady pull (by raising his heel) and to repeat the pull several times. This "intermittent traction" will relieve neck tension by alternately stretching and releasing the neck muscles. It's very important to sit perfectly straight while receiving the traction so that your spine won't be so slack that it's difficult to stretch your neck muscles.

NECK TRACTION ON THE JOB: I once recommended the partner method of traction for a shirt-factory seamstress who complained of headache and tired neck muscles. When I saw her several months later, she told me that the traction was so effective that she recommended it to several of her co-workers. Now, whenever they take a coffee break, they all take turns stretching each other's neck.

Relief of neck tension with traction is very often immediate, as indicated by the expressions of persons who say "my head sure feels lighter." It's not at all uncommon for a patient to say that he can "see better" immediately following partner-type neck traction. I have always attributed this to an increase in the flow of blood through previously tight neck muscles, thus increasing the flow of blood to the brain.

RELIEVING ARM AND SHOULDER PAIN WITH TRACTION: Neck traction can be used to relieve arm and shoulder pain as well as headache and nervous tension. The nerves supplying your arms pass out from between the vertebrae in the lower part of your neck to reach down into your fingertips. If one of these nerves is irritated to cause numbness, tingling, or pain in some portion of your shoulder, arm, or hand, the symptoms can very often be relieved by applying traction that's heavy enough to separate the vertebrae of the neck a little. Traction for this purpose is usually best applied for several minutes at a time with a head harness.

C.   **TRACTION WITH A HEAD HARNESS:**   If none of the other methods of traction seem to relieve your neck tension or your headache, or if you'd rather use continuous traction without depending upon aid from your friends, you can stretch your neck with a head harness. Any surgical or orthopedic supply store can furnish you with "cervical traction" equipment, along with complete instructions on how to use it.

Doorway traction in a sitting position will be most convenient for the average person. A head harness is strapped under the chin and around the base of the skull. A cord attached to the harness is then passed over a couple of pulleys that are secured to a metal arm projecting out from the top of the door. A weight is fastened to the end of the cord so that it will hang suspended next to the door. While applying the traction, you sit with your back to the door, with the weight behind you, so that the cord attached to the harness will pull in line with your spine. (See Figure 3-4.)

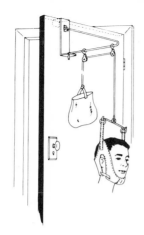

Figure 3-4. *Persons who travel or live alone can relieve tension headache with a traction harness.*

For simple muscular tension, five or ten minutes of traction with seven to ten pounds of weight should be adequate. In some cases, however, 15 or 20 pounds for only a few minutes at a time will produce better results.

Always try the lighter weight first. If you go to a heavier weight, don't use so much that you tense your neck muscles in resisting the pull. It's important that you relax completely so that the muscles of your neck will "give" to the pull. Sit in a straight-back chair so that you can lean backward a little and sit relaxed with a straight spine.

ANYONE CAN USE TRACTION SAFELY: There is absolutely no danger in the proper use of cervical traction. It can be used safely by anyone not suffering from a diseased or injured spine. In fact, properly applied, it should be relaxing and comfortable. *Discontinue the traction if you should feel any pain or discomfort.*

PORTABLE CERVICAL TRACTION: Doorway traction equipment is so light and easy to carry around that it may be installed on any door anywhere. A tension-harassed businessman can use it in his office. A headache-plagued housewife can use it at home. A traveling salesman can carry his around and install it on a door wherever he may be. I wouldn't advise taking traction in public, however, since onlookers may view you with something less than curiosity.

A tension-ridden grammar school teacher installed her cervical traction equipment on the back of a cloakroom door. Every time she feels her neck muscles tighten up from a build-up of tension, she prevents development of tension headache by using the traction for 10 or 15 minutes.

If you do carry your traction equipment from one place to another, you can use a collapsible water bag for weight if you don't want to lug solid weights around. Most surgical supply stores sell such bags. You simply fill the bag with water, to the level indicating the weight you want, and then attach it to your traction cord. When the traction is finished, you can empty the bag and fold it up until you need it again.

If you use your traction only at home, a canvas bag filled with non-dusty builder's sand (and sewed shut) makes a good weight. Fill two or three bags in weights ranging from seven to 20 pounds.

2.   Drive Out the Soreness with Moist Heat

Whenever the muscles of your neck are sore and inflamed from prolonged tension or spasm, simple moist heat should provide some immediate relief.

Try standing under a shower and letting a thick stream of hot water play over the muscles of your neck and shoulders, or wring out a towel in hot water and drape it over the back of your neck. Since a hot towel cools rapidly, it must be reapplied several times in order to maintain the heat. If you have an infrared heat lamp or an insulated heating pad, you can keep a moist towel hot by heating it after it has been applied to your neck.

With a little ingenuity, you can devise a variety of ways to apply moist heat. See Chapter 9 for additional suggestions on the use of heat.

DON'T DELAY: It's important to begin the use of moist heat as soon as you become aware of unrelieved muscle tension in your neck. An attorney who "toughed it out" during a difficult three-week court trial ended up in the hospital when his fatigued and spastic neck muscles could no longer hold his head up. Had he taken time to do nothing more than apply hot towels to his neck, he could probably have avoided the acute reaction of inflammatory muscle spasm.

3.   Loosen the Muscles with Massage

Light massage is always helpful in relieving muscle tightness and soreness. But a special technique must be used to knead the muscles on the back of the neck. And since most of the tension in tight neck muscles is felt at the top of the neck where the muscles attach to the base of the skull, it is here that you should apply the massage. (See Figure 3-5.)

A MASSAGE TECHNIQUE THAT ANYONE CAN USE: Try this method of massage on a friend and then let him try it on you. Have the "patient" sit on a low stool or chair. Then place your left hand (if you're right handed) on his forehead so that you can support his head when he tilts it forward. It's important for the patient to let his head rest against your hand so that the muscles on the back of his neck will be completely relaxed. Encircle the back of his neck (where it joins his head) with the thumb and forefinger of

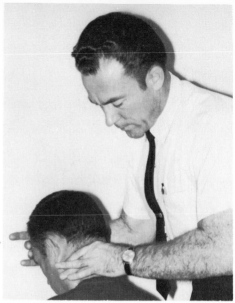

Figure 3-5. Neck massage should be applied at the top of the neck near the base of the skull.

your right hand. Massage the neck by moving the massaging hand up and down in a circular motion.

Be sure to press the massaging hand firmly against the neck so that it will stay in contact with the skin as it rides over the muscles. In other words, don't let your hand slide over the skin to create an uncomfortable friction. The muscle attachments at the top of the neck can be massaged more effectively by using short circular strokes that move only as far as looseness of the skin will permit.

Simply placing pressure on each side of the neck just beneath the skull will sometimes relieve headache by relaxing nerves and muscles.

If you want to employ long, stroking massage over the skin, it'll be necessary to apply some kind of oil to the subject's neck to prevent excessive friction.

It isn't necessary or even desirable to employ any other type of massage to the neck. Don't ever attempt to hack the muscles of the neck. You might inadvertently administer a "karate chop" and have a casualty on your hands —or you might disturb an arthritic process in the joints of the cervical spine.

4. Relieving Head Pain with an Ice Pack

Once a headache does develop and none of the other measures seem to help, try using an ice pack. Since the pain in the majority of headaches is caused by dilatation (expansion) of the blood vessels around the brain, a cold pack will help relieve the symptoms by constricting the swollen vessels.

If the application doesn't seem to be effective on your forehead or on the top of your head, place it on the front of your neck for several minutes. Chill-

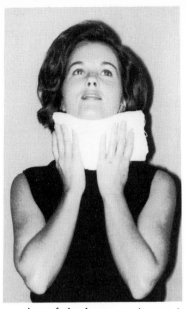

Figure 3-6. An ice pack applied to the front of the neck will sometimes relieve. a severe headache.

ing of the large arteries passing through the neck to the brain will reflexly relieve the pressure in the arteries around the brain. (See Figure 3-6.)

THE "SLEEPER HOLD" FOR HEADACHES: Putting a little manual pressure on the carotid arteries in your neck will also reduce the amount of blood flowing to your brain to relieve the pressure in painfully dilated arteries. You can find these arteries by locating your "heart beat" on each side of the front of your neck. Don't maintain the pressure for longer than about three seconds at a time, however, since blackout could occur from obstruction of blood flow to the brain.

Whenever pressure is exerted on the junction of the arteries at the bottom of the neck (carotid sinus) for very long, the blood pressure drops and the heart rate slows down. This is why some people faint when they wear a tight collar.

You can also reduce your blood pressure and slow your heart rate by putting a little pressure on the far side of each eyeball. This is the result of a nervous system reflex that signals the heart and the vascular system. Most people will instinctively reach up and place a thumb and forefinger against their closed eyelids whenever headache or nervous tension overtakes them. (See Figure 3-7.)

COLD FOOT BATHS: A cold foot bath with water cooled to 50 to 70 degrees Fahrenheit will sometimes relieve headache by causing reflex constriction of the blood vessels around the brain.

HOT FOOT BATHS: "Congestive headaches" caused by cold infection or allergy can be relieved better by taking a hot foot bath while applying an ice bag to the head.

Figure 3-7. Light pressure on the eyeballs might be effective in relieving headache caused by high blood pressure.

5. Using Aspirin and Coffee for Medicinal Purposes

Simple aspirin, if not taken excessively, is one of the safest home medications known for relief of pain. Manufactured originally by boiling the bark of a willow tree to obtain a substance called "salicin," aspirin is now composed of a synthetic substance called "acetylsalicylic acid."

USING ASPIRIN AS A HEADACHE DRUG: You should avoid the use of any kind of medicines and drugs whenever possible. But if you develop a splitting headache that cannot be relieved by natural means, the relief provided by an aspirin or two can be a godsend, and it may be just as effective as some of the more powerful drugs.

SIDE EFFECTS OF ASPIRIN: Even aspirin can have side effects, however. Medical scientists tell us that the ingredients of aspirin tend to break down red blood cells and erode the lining of the stomach. So don't take it unless you feel you have to, and then don't take it any longer than necessary. Persons who "eat aspirin" day after day are greatly endangering their health, and they get less relief from pain than persons who take aspirin only occasionally.

When you feel you need medication for relief of pain, always try aspirin before asking your doctor for potentially dangerous narcotics. It's not necessary to take more than two aspirin at a time, since no greater relief from pain would result.

If you make use of the self-help techniques outlined in this chapter for relief of simple tension headache, you probably won't ever have to take an aspirin. For your health's sake, try the natural way first. And remember that taking pain relievers will not remove the cause of your headache.

HOW TO MAKE YOUR OWN ASPIRIN: If you don't want to take synthetic aspirin, you can make your own by steeping half an ounce of willow bark in three cups of boiling water and then letting it stand overnight before boiling it for a full five minutes. You may also mix two teaspoons of powdered willow bark in three cups of boiling water and then let it stand for eight hours. In either case, you drink the solution for pain-relieving effects.

COFFEE AS A PAIN RELIEVER: The caffeine in a cup of coffee will sometimes relieve headache in persons who aren't heavy coffee drinkers. Caffeine is a "vasoconstrictor," which means that it constricts blood vessels. This would tend to relieve headache in which pain is caused by swollen arteries.

Persons who become "addicted" to daily and excessive use of coffee as a beverage sometimes develop headache as a "withdrawal symptom" whenever they skip their usual cup of coffee.

Excessive use of coffee can make you nervous and irritable, and it can keep you awake at night. Caffeine is a powerful stimulant, and it acts very much like a drug.

COMBINING ASPIRIN AND COFFEE: If neither aspirin nor a cup of coffee seems to relieve your headache, try taking them together. Aspirin as a pain killer and coffee as a vasoconstrictor will attack your headache with double strength. Whenever a headache persists or recurs, it's always a good idea to see a doctor in order to make sure that it isn't something more serious than a tension headache.

WHAT TO DO ABOUT MIGRAINE

Whenever a recurring headache of unknown cause is accompanied by nausea, vomiting, visual disturbances, shock, and other symptoms of illness, it is usually called "sick headache" or "migraine." Little is known about this type of headache. Most doctors believe that it is inherited, just as one inherits epilepsy. There is reason to believe that sensitive, high-strung persons are more subject to migraine than other persons. There seems to be little doubt that it can be triggered by nervous tension. Be sure to read Chapter 2 if you suffer from "nerves."

Why Migraine Is so Painful

Like many other types of headaches, the pain of migraine is caused by dilation (expanding) of the blood vessels. In "sick headaches," however, the pain is much more severe, since the arteries have been sensitized by chemical changes in the blood. There is usually no evidence of organic illness. Persons who suffer from migraine may be perfectly normal and healthy between attacks.

The Premonition of Migraine

A true migraine headache is usually preceded by a warning or "premonition" which medical men call an "aura." This is believed to be caused by constriction of the blood vessels just before they dilate.

Some migraine sufferers experience numbness, nausea, weakness, or great excitement. Some see "spots." A few see half of everything, just as if their field of vision had been cut in half. When the headache begins, it is usually on one side of the head. A swollen, throbbing artery can sometimes be seen on the painful side of the forehead.

How to Relieve the Pain of Migraine

At the present time, there does not appear to be any sure way to prevent or cure true migraine headache. Complete rest in a dark room, with a cold pack on the head or the neck, may relieve the symptoms to some extent. Some sufferers maintain that they can abort the headache by having a bowel movement or by taking an enema whenever the preliminary symptoms appear. (See Chapter 4 for enema technique and for an explanation of how constipation can cause headache.) Wrapping a bandage tightly around the head above the eyes seems to help in some cases.

SPECIAL MEDICATION FOR SEVERE MIGRAINE: When simple physical treatment does not relieve a migraine headache, a physician can prescribe special drugs that will relieve the symptoms by constricting the sensitized arteries around the brain. In some cases, the headache can be prevented by taking the drugs when an aura warns of an oncoming attack. Use of these drugs should be discontinued, however, if the individual finds that he is allergic to them or that he develops serious side effects.

Antihistamine, such as that found in common cold remedies, will sometimes relieve headaches caused by histamine allergy. If your headache is accompanied by watery eyes, ask your doctor about a "histamine check."

HEADACHE CURED BY MENOPAUSE: Whenever migraine occurs with menstruation, treatment with hormones might help. In such cases, menopause often "cures" the headache. The chemical changes of age may also be a factor in relief from migraine, since the disorder often disappears after 50 years of age.

Maybe You Have "False Migraine"

Persons who suffer from "pseudomigraine," a simple tension headache that is so severe that it resembles true migraine, can very often get relief from the use of such simple physical treatment as traction. For this reason, you might try the self-help techniques recommended for tension headache, even if your headache has been diagnosed as "migraine."

Loosening the muscles and vertebrae of the neck with manipulation, or "adjustment" of the spine, is often very effective in relieving tension headache—or any headache not caused by organic disease.

Medical scientists have discovered that prolonged contraction of the muscles of the neck and scalp can release "headache chemicals" into the blood, as well as irritate nerves, obstruct blood circulation, and pull the bones of the neck out of alignment.

Tension Headache Caused by Migraine

Migraine headaches are often so severe that they trigger a tension headache that persists long after the "sick headache" is over. For this reason, it's always a good idea to apply physical treatment to the muscles of the neck during and after the attack, even if it does nothing for migraine itself.

OTHER CAUSES OF HEADACHE

There are many causes of headache. Eye strain, glaucoma, sinus infection, loss of sleep, fatigue, allergy, fever, high blood pressure, brain tumor, emotional strain, and constipation, for example, must be considered in some cases.

There are some doctors who believe that eye-muscle fatigue and constipation are the two most common causes of headache. Others believe that fatigue and nervous tension should head the list. It's the general consensus, however, that prolonged contraction of the muscles of the neck is responsible for most headaches—and this is most often the result of fatigue produced by working postures or nervous tension produced by a state of mind. A person in the throes of great distress may hold his neck muscles so rigid that he develops a headache that is much more severe than that produced by simple mechanical strain.

HEADACHE CAUSED BY ORGANIC DISEASE IS RARE: Fortunately, headache is rarely caused by serious organic disease. So you don't need to get unduly alarmed every time your head aches. But if you should suddenly develop a severe head pain, or if your headache should persist unrelieved, be sure to see your doctor. Any headache accompanied by other symptoms, such as fever or difficulty in breathing, points to possible allergy or organic disease. See your doctor immediately if you should develop a headache following a blow on your head.

An Example of Fatal Headache

Not all serious or fatal headaches are caused by blows, infection, or organic disease. I know of one case where a man was suddenly stricken with a severe head pain while walking down the street.

"The pain struck like the blow of a sledge hammer," he said, "and it was so severe that I was out of my head for awhile."

He refused to seek medical care, however; and when he returned to work a few days later, he died from cerebral hemorrhage. It seems that the man was suffering from cerebral aneurysm, which means that a weak artery had suddenly ballooned out like a weak spot on an inflated inner tube. Lack of adequate rest and medication to reduce his blood pressure had resulted in rupture of the swollen artery.

A Case of Emotional Headache

It is not at all uncommon for persons with emotional problems or difficult-to-face life situations to suffer from chronic headache as an escape mechanism. And until every possible organic cause is eliminated, it's sometimes difficult for the doctor as well as the patient to accept the fact that the headache is entirely mental in origin.

One young lady who came to me complaining of headache obtained some relief from manipulation and other methods of treatment designed to relieve tense muscles and nerves. But when the headache persisted, I sent her back to her family physician who concurred with my recommendation that she see a neurologist or "nerve specialist." When his examination failed to reveal any organic disease, he questioned her closely about her personal life and found that she was distressed and "humiliated" because of her father's confinement for alcoholism. She had refused to admit to me or her family physician that she had any emotional problems. When she finally brought her troubles into the open by discussing them with the out-of-town doctor, she learned that her father was suffering from an illness that she need not be ashamed of. Her headache gradually disappeared.

The point to be made in this example is that one of the most effective treatments for ills of emotional origin is "mental catharsis"—that is, talking out your troubles with someone you respect and trust and with whom you know your "secret" is safe. In many cases, competent consultation will completely eliminate bottled-up tension by erasing false conceptions.

Impure Air Can Cause Headache

If you live or work in the city, you may suffer from headache caused by lack of fresh air. Excessive amounts of carbon monoxide in the air—from engines and heaters—can deprive your brain of oxygen by invading your blood stream. Whenever this is the case, a little fresh air provides immediate relief.

Unfortunately, the air in our cities is filled with excessive amounts of carbon monoxide, especially in areas where auto traffic is heavy and where the air is hazy with industrial fumes and smoke. If you work in an area where the air is contaminated, try to take a "fresh air break" periodically so that you can go somewhere and fill your lungs with clean air. Traffic policemen and highway tunnel workers, for example, should not be forced to stay on the job for too long at a stretch.

See Chapter 14 for additional tips on breathing.

Check the Exhaust Pipe on Your Car

If you should ever develop a headache while riding in a closed car, lower a window and then have the car's exhaust pipe checked for leaks. This could save your life as well as prevent a recurrence of headache.

Balancing Your Sugar Intake to Prevent Headache

Low blood sugar from missing a meal or two can cause headache that can be relieved by eating. If you get hungry between meals and develop a headache as a result, try a little snack of fresh or dried fruits to tide you over. Such protein-rich foods as nuts, cheese and crackers, and sunflower seeds are also great for boosting energy stores and satisfying hunger.

Excessive use of refined sugar will overstimulate your body's production of insulin, which will result in a "sugar hangover" from a sudden drop in blood sugar a few hours later. The insulin-producing cells of the pancreas may also be overworked to contribute to the development of diabetes.

Persons who are constantly eating candy for "energy" may feel more tired and headachy at the end of the day than persons who eat nothing at all between meals. If you'll eat a good, protein-rich breakfast each morning, chances are you'll have enough energy to carry you from one meal to the next.

A piece of fresh citrus fruit or a handful of cold grapes first thing in the morning will give you a refreshing lift. Honey on a slice of pure whole-wheat bread will give you a nourishing boost late in the afternoon when tension headache and low energy stores begin to drag you down.

Alcohol Depletes Energy Stores to Cause Headache

Excessive use of alcohol can disturb the body's use of sugar by "hogging" the liver. Normally the liver converts simple sugars into glycogen so they can be used by the muscles for energy. But when this important organ is forced to cleanse the blood by burning alcohol, it cannot maintain the body's energy stores. Insulin, Vitamin B, Vitamin C, and glucose are also wasted.

Calories supplied by alcohol cannot be stored in the body. An alcoholic can get some immediate energy from alcoholic beverages, but when the drinking is discontinued he suffers from headache, nervousness, and other symptoms characteristic of a "hangover" or depleted energy stores.

Headache Caused by a Reversed Neck Curve

In treating patients for chronic headache in my own practice, I've noticed that a great many of them have a "reversed cervical curve." In other words, instead of the cervical (neck) spine curving forward as it should, the curve either straightens or reverses so that its convexity is directed backward instead of forward. Outwardly, the neck appears to be normal, but the muscles of the neck must work in supporting the head. This results in chronic tension headache from the constant pull of muscles attaching to the base of the skull.

In many cases, reversal of the cervical curve is caused by degeneration of discs and other disturbances in the spine. But it may also result from years of unrelieved neck tension. In either case, an effort should be made to restore the normal curve with special exercises.

ALIGNING YOUR NECK WITH EXERCISE: You can strengthen the muscles supporting your neck, as well as restore its normal curve, by taking one simple exercise. Lock your fingers behind your head and then tilt your head back against resistance applied by your hands. Do several repetitions at least once a day. Make sure the exercise is isotonic rather than isometric; that is, begin with your neck erect and then extend it back as far as you can. (See Figure 3-8.)

Even if your neck is normal, you can do this exercise in order to make sure that it stays normal. Regular exercise of the neck muscles will maintain their

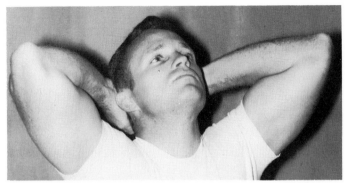

Figure 3-8. Extend your head back against the resistance of your hands and inhale deeply.

tone and flush out irritating deposits by pumping blood through them. Whenever the muscles on the back of the neck are spongy and lumpy from lack of exercise, they can trigger a chronic headache that cannot be cured without special exercises.

If you have a lot of "cricks" or muscle spasms in your neck, you can exercise your neck more effectively by lifting a little weight with your head. Secure a weight to the ends of a large towel and then drape it over your head. Exercise your neck by leaning forward and bracing your hands on your knees so that you can lift the weight up and down with your neck muscles. Do 12 to 15 repetitions. For weight, try using a handbag containing a brick. This is an excellent exercise for mechanical correction of your neck. (See Figure 3-9.)

SUPPORTING YOUR NECK WITH A PILLOW

If the normal curve of your neck spine has reversed itself to any degree, it will tend to sag into even more reversal when you support the back of your head with a pillow. You can guard against this by making sure that the pillow also supports the back of your neck. (See Figure 3-10.)

Use a thin pillow under your head so that your head will rest in line with the rest of your body, but fluff up the bottom edge of the pillow so that it will fit into the hollow beneath your neck. This will relieve strain on the joints and ligaments and permit you to relax better for a good night's sleep.

AVOID THE USE OF FOAM RUBBER PILLOWS: Always use firmly packed feather pillows whenever you have a choice. Springy foam-rubber pillows may contribute to development of neck tension and headache by failing to offer solid support for your head.

Figure 3-9. Regular resistive isotonic neck exercise will maintain the normal curve of the neck spine.

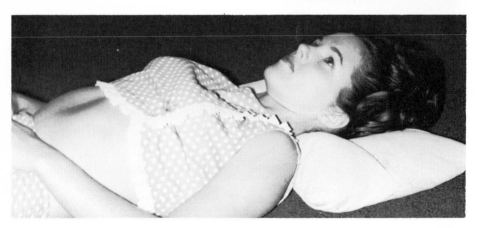

Figure 3-10. When lying down, support the back of your neck with the bottom edge of your pillow.

SUMMARY

1. Simple home-treatment techniques that are designed to relax tight muscles on the back of the head and neck will cure or relieve most headaches.

2. Light traction on the muscles of the neck has been found to be effective in relieving muscular tension and the dull ache of tension headache.

3. Simple moist heat and massage applied to the muscles of the neck can be used to relieve soreness and stiffness caused by prolonged tension.

4. A cold pack applied to the head or the neck will relieve the pain of a throbbing headache by constricting dilated blood vessels.

5. An aspirin or a cup of coffee, or both together, is sometimes effective in relieving tension headache that cannot be relieved with physical treatment.

6. When you go to bed each night, try to maintain the normal curve of your cervical spine by supporting the back of your neck with a fluffed-up portion of your pillow.

7. Face life's problems squarely and realistically in order to prevent bottled-up tensions. Always take a little time for relaxing and entertaining pastimes for better nervous and mental health.

8. Be sure to study all the other chapters in this book for additional health-building tips that will help you prevent headache.

4

Rid Yourself of Constipation

Constipation is so common in the United States that it is sometimes called the "Great American Disease." The sale of laxatives is such a big business that TV and radio commercials exploiting the bowel movements of young and old alike are as commonplace as soap sales and soup ads. Americans respond to these sales pitches by spending millions of dollars a year on all kinds of laxatives. The result is that constipation has become more of a problem than ever, and the disease is made worse rather than better.

There are natural ways to rid yourself of constipation, however. And in the process, you can improve your health. This treasure can be yours simply by following certain rules set out in this chapter. This chapter outlines a safe and effective self-help program that anyone can use to relieve or prevent constipation.

DON'T BE A VICTIM OF IMAGINARY CONSTIPATION

Although constipation is a legitimate complaint in a "civilized" country where refined and processed food items make up a large portion of the average person's diet, many people who take laxatives are not really constipated —at least they weren't before they started taking laxatives. Most of us have been led to believe that it is absolutely necessary to have at least one bowel movement each day, lest we become "poisoned" by intestinal toxins.

Actually, no real harm would result from failure to have a bowel movement for a couple of days. Prolonged retention of the stool would cause constipation by allowing the contents of the lower colon to harden from absorption of water, but no poisoning would occur.

Some doctors still maintain that retention of waste matter in the colon may contribute to the development of arthritis and similar disorders. Most disagree. All do agree, however, that chronic constipation is unhealthy, and that every effort should be made to make sure that the bowels move regularly.

Whatever effect constipation might have can be eliminated by observing the rules outlined in this chapter. You don't have to suffer from that bloated, headachy feeling that constipated people complain about.

DON'T TAKE LAXATIVES OUT OF PANIC

You should, of course, try to have a bowel movement every day. But if you fail to do so for a couple of days, you shouldn't panic and take a high-powered laxative. This would only overstimulate your bowels and leave them more lifeless than ever after they have been forcefully emptied.

Many people who take laxatives fail to realize that once the intestinal tract has been purged, it may take several days for enough waste matter to accumulate in the lower bowel to create an urge to visit the toilet. As a result, they become impatient after a couple of days and take another laxative. This leads to chronic constipation that is *caused* by the use of laxatives!

Once the bowels become accustomed to being triggered into action by intestinal irritants (laxatives), they become more lazy and require progressively stronger laxatives to make them move. They literally become addicted to laxatives. The whole digestive system is upset. Food may be only partially digested in a slow-moving intestinal tract that's periodically whipped into action.

HOW OFTEN SHOULD YOUR BOWELS MOVE?

Most people have one or two bowel movements every day; others may go every-other-day or less. It may be perfectly normal for some individuals to empty their bowels only once or twice a week. The important thing is to determine what is or is not normal for you. Then, if your regularity is disturbed, you can take some additional action to help your bowels along.

When the bowels are tardy, they will usually move normally if certain simple rules of diet and exercise are observed. In some cases, the accumulation of hardened waste matter in the colon will trigger a cleansing diarrhea. Nature has a way of taking care of your body functions if you only observe her laws. But if you allow chronic constipation to develop from bad living habits, and you don't make an effort to change your way of life, you're headed for trouble—in more ways than one.

A CASE HISTORY OF CONSTIPATION

The history of Malcolm E. is typical of patients who suffer from constipation caused by bad living habits. Until he graduated from college, he never had any difficulty with his bowels, and he never took enemas or laxatives. But not long after he began working as a sales manager for an auto dealer, his troubles began. And after a couple of years in what he called the "automotive rat race," he was taking laxatives regularly. I found that he was completely ignorant of the cause of his constipation, and he felt that he could not get by without taking laxatives regularly.

It seems that Malcolm was a heavy sleeper, and very often he failed to get up in time to eat breakfast and sit on the toilet. When lunch time rolled around, he frequently ate "only a sandwich" so that he could get back to "pressing business." He insisted that he did not have time to "sit around in the toilet." If he did feel an urge during working hours, he'd postpone it until a more convenient time. When he finally did get a little "free time," he no longer felt an urge to go; and no matter how long he sat on the toilet, nothing happened.

After three or four days, usually on the weekends, Malcolm E. would take a strong laxative. This usually resulted in a heavy action on Sunday morning. Then, if his bowels didn't move again after a couple of days, he'd take another laxative "just to keep them moving." Under these conditions he was doomed to suffer from chronic constipation and all the discomforts and inconveniences that go along with it.

I took this patient off laxatives and suggested that he follow the recommendations outlined in this chapter. He took my advice, and after several weeks was once again having normal, healthy bowel movements. His headaches and nervousness disappeared, and he claimed to be as alert and energetic as he once was during his school days.

If you suffer from constipation and its side effects, you can do as much for yourself as Malcolm E. did by taking the same course of action I recommend for all my patients who complain of "sluggish bowels."

THREE TYPES OF CONSTIPATION

Basically, there are three types of constipation: atonic, spastic, and obstructive. The atonic type is by far the most common. In this condition, the colon is simply lazy or tardy. There is no pain or illness, just lack of movement.

In spastic constipation, there is pain with abdominal cramps. In the obstructive type, fever and other symptoms of illness will be evident. If you're over 50 years of age, any change in bowel habits that persists for longer than two weeks should be brought to the attention of your family doctor.

For self-help purposes, we'll be concerned only with atonic constipation. *If your constipation is associated with pain or illness, see your doctor.*

CAUSES OF ATONIC CONSTIPATION

Although improper diet is a major factor in constipation, there are many contributing causes. Lack of exercise, irregular toilet habits, omission of regular meals, use of laxatives, not drinking enough water, and irregular working and sleeping hours, for example, can all play a part in chronic constipation.

HOW TO ELIMINATE COMMON CAUSES OF CONSTIPATION

Eliminating the causes of constipation will also improve your general health. Here are some important guidelines that you should not fail to observe in taking care of your bowels.

1. Put a Little Roughage in Your Diet

The highly refined and starchy foods that lead to Vitamin B deficiency and nervous symptoms are also deficient in the roughage needed to stimulate action in the intestional tract. If you don't include fruits and vegetables in your diet each day, you're almost sure to suffer from constipation.

FOODS RICH IN CELLULOSE: All kinds of vegetables, such as asparagus, spinach, turnips, tomatoes, and cauliflower, are rich in cellulose, which acts as a roughage. Try to eat servings of at least two different vegetables each day.

DON'T PEEL YOUR FRUITS AND VEGETABLES: Unpeeled fresh and dried fruits, such as apples, peaches, pears, prunes, dates, figs, and raisins, also leave an indigestible residue in the intestines. Try to eat a piece of fresh fruit and several pieces of dried fruit each evening.

Always wash your fruit with soap and water if you plan to eat the skin. Many fruits, such as apples, pick up a greasy film that cannot be washed off with plain water. Some stores actually spray their fruit and vegetable displays with oily insecticides.

People once believed that you must be able to digest everything you eat. Many of them would discard the pulp of an orange or the peeling of a potato. The truth is, however, that if you don't include some indigestible foods in your diet, there won't be enough bulk in your bowels to form a firm and easily passable stool.

Whenever possible, you should also eat the skins of vegetables. Most of them are edible, as well as nourishing. The skin of a baked Irish potato, for example, is very tasty, and it contains vitamins and minerals as well as roughage. You don't have to go to all the trouble of peeling potatoes, scraping carrots, and so on. But you should wash them thoroughly before cooking or eating them.

SUPPLEMENTING YOUR DIET WITH AGAR-AGAR: Many "city folks" who subsist largely on sandwiches and beverages also eat agar-agar, an indigestible seaweed product that can be flavored and cooked as jelly or made into biscuits. Cellulose tablets and a gelatinous-like extract from psyllium seed are also good sources of bulk. Shredded wheat wafers will provide bulk as well as intestinal stimulation.

Try to get your bulk from natural health-building foods rather than from synthetic products that swell up in your stomach to kill your appetite. Whenever you're unable to get adequate amounts of fruits and vegetables, your health food store can supply you with a bulk supplement.

BRAN AS AN INTESTINAL STIMULANT: If you eat cereals, always select those that contain bran, such as rolled oats, cut oats, cut wheat, brown rice, and shredded wheat. Don't buy the refined, puffed-up cereals that no longer resemble the whole grains they were made from.

Pure whole wheat bread also contains bran. One of my patients, an 84-year-old Swede, believes that his daily diet of homemade whole wheat bread enables him to continue in his occupation as a boat builder. He claims that he never has trouble with his bowels.

WARNING: If you should develop diarrhea, colitis, or some other gastrointestinal or colon disorder, see your doctor. You may have to discontinue the use of roughage and adopt a special bland or soft diet until your trouble is corrected. Many elderly persons suffer from "diverticulitis," which is an inflammation of tiny pouches in the walls of the colon. Whenever cellulose or bran becomes lodged in these pouches, diarrhea occurs. If this continues unchecked, dehydration and other disturbances may occur.

2. Drink Plenty of Water

Drink several glasses of water each day—or an equivalent amount of fruit juice, milk, and other liquids—so that your stools will be moist rather than dry. Your body absorbs a great deal of water from all portions of your intestinal tract, so it is necessary to drink more water than your body can use in order for enough to get through to soften the waste matter in your colon.

It's all right to drink liquids with your meals as long as you don't use them to wash down unchewed food.

A LEMON LAXATIVE: A glass of warm water with the juice of a lemon first thing in the morning may help stimulate a before-breakfast bowel movement. The organic acid in any type of fruit juice will help abolish constipation by stimulating the muscular action of the intestines.

Many people experience the urge to defecate or empty their bowels after their usual early-morning cup of coffee.

3. Schedule Your Meals

Try to eat your meals at the same time each day. This will make it easier to move your bowels at an appointed time.

If your bowels don't move every time you expect them to, don't worry about it. Chances are they'll move during your next scheduled toilet appointment —if they don't move before then—if your meals are regular.

There are many factors, such as emotional stress or a change in daily routine, that will throw your bowels a little off schedule from time to time. When this happens, you should heed the "urge" whenever and wherever it occurs, while still observing your regular eating and toilet schedules.

4. Establish Regular Toilet Hours

Regardless of how good your diet may be, you must not fail to visit the toilet at the same time each day if you want to avoid constipation. Whenever you deliberately postpone an urge to empty your bowels, your body may absorb enough water from the contents of the lower colon to leave them hard and lumpy. This will obstruct the bowels to cause an uncomfortable form of constipation. Furthermore, when you consistently ignore the call of nature, the urge may diminish or disappear, letting the colon enlarge excessively from overloading.

If your bowels fail to move after a couple of days, increase your intake of water and roughage. If you find it necessary to take an enema after three or four days, try to take it during the time you would normally have a bowel movement.

WHAT CONSTIPATION CAN DO TO YOU: Distension of the lower bowel from impaction of waste matter can result in headaches, mental confusion, sluggishness, and other disturbances—not from poisoning, but from reflex symptoms caused by stretching of the nerves and blood vessels in the walls of the colon. Doctors have reproduced such symptoms by stuffing the rectum with cotton. (You learned in Chapter 3 that persons who suffer from migraine can sometimes abort a headache by emptying their bowels whenever the first symptoms of headache appear.)

If you get in such a hurry each day that you don't take time to visit the toilet at appointed times, you may find yourself suffering from headache if not from embarrassing and explosive urges that compel you to run to the toilet at the most inopportune times.

5. Don't Rush Your Bowels

When you do sit on the toilet, take the time you need to have a good bowel movement. The passing of waste matter from one portion of the colon to another in the process of emptying the bowels depends largely upon a muscular wave-like action in the walls of the intestinal tract. Called "peristalsis," this action pushes waste matter along to the point of evacuation; it cannot be hurried.

STRAINING CAN CAUSE HEMORRHOIDS: Trying to speed evacuation by straining too vigorously can aggravate or cause hemorrhoids or a hernia— or both. The increased abdominal pressure will obstruct the venous blood flow and cause the rectal veins to swell. If you do attempt to empty your bowels forcefully, don't hold your breath in the process. Always exhale when you strain.

See Chapter 11 for an explanation of how straining and breath-holding can cause hernia.

6. How to Massage Your Colon for Better Bowel Function

If you have difficulty with your bowels in spite of good living habits, you may be able to encourage their function by massaging your colon or by vibrating the nerves in the lower part of your back. Such mechanical stimulation has proven to be very effective in some otherwise very stubborn cases.

TECHNIQUE OF MASSAGING THE COLON: If you remember your high school biology, you know that the eliminating portion of your lower intestinal tract is divided into three portions. One portion travels up the right side of your abdomen, the second across the top of your abdomen from right to left, the third down the left side of your abdomen.

You can push the contents of the colon along in a sort of "mechanical peristalsis" by following its course with overlapping and circular massaging movements.

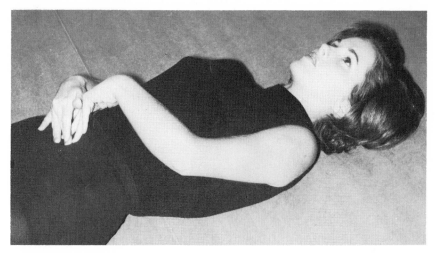

Figure 4-1. *To massage your colon, begin on the lower right hand side of your abdomen and then follow a course up and around the abdomen.*

Lie on your back so that your abdominal muscles will be relaxed. Start the massage in the lower right hand corner of your abdomen and work your way up, across, and down the other side of your abdomen. You may use the fingertips of one or both hands. Don't use so much pressure that you experience any pain or discomfort. Repeat the massage three or four times each day, or before each visit to the toilet. (See Figure 4-1.)

TECHNIQUE OF VIBRATING THE NERVES: The nerves supplying the colon can be stimulated mechanically by applying vibration over the sacrum on the back of the pelvis. This can be done with a machine vibrator or by hand. In either case, it must be applied by a partner.

Lie face down and instruct your partner to apply the vibrator over the flat surface of your pelvis between the dimples just above your buttocks.

The vibration may be applied manually by laying two fingers over the sacrum and pounding them gently with the bottom side of a clenched fist. (See Figure 4-2.)

7. Two Simple Exercises for Better Bowel Function

Regular abdominal exercise can be just as important for good bowel health as for a trim waistline. Any exercise that calls for contraction of the abdominal muscles and bending of the trunk will improve the tone of the bowels. The pressure placed upon the abdominal organs by contracting muscles will also tend to push the contents of the colon into the rectum.

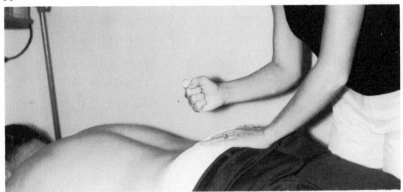

Figure 4-2. Pelvic nerves can be stimulated by placing two fingers over the lower spine and then lightly pounding them with the bottom of a closed fist.

THE SIMPLE SIT-UP is one of the best abdominal exercises. Lie on your back on a rug with your knees bent, your hands behind your head, and your feet anchored under the edge of a heavy sofa. Sit up by curling your head and shoulders up from the floor so that you can touch your elbows to your knees. Begin by doing only a few repetitions, and then work up to 12 or more over a period of time. (See Figure 4-3.)

If you aren't able to do a sit-up, curl only your head and shoulders up from the floor as in beginning a sit-up. Then gradually work up to regular sit-ups. The abdominal-lift exercises described in Chapter 14 will also stimulate bowel function.

Figure 4-3. Simple sit-up exercises help to stimulate bowel function.

BENT-KNEE LEG RAISES should also be included in your exercise program. Lie on your back with your hands palms-down on the rug alongside your body and your knees bent so that the soles of your feet are flat on the rug. Holding your knees in this bent position, lift them up toward your chest as far as you can. As you do, press down against the rug with your hands so that you can curl your pelvis up from the floor. Do as many repetitions as you comfortably can.

Try to take your exercises every day, preferably before your evening meal. Remember that it's important to keep the abdomen muscular and flat. Once you develop a "pot belly," sagging abdominal organs will squeeze the life out of your intestinal tract.

HOW TO BREATHE DURING YOUR EXERCISES: Don't hold your breath during sit-ups and leg raises. Exhale during the active part of these exercises or while contracting the abdominal muscles. Turn to Chapter 11 and study the breathing techniques recommended for prevention of hernia.

8. Avoid Nervous Tension and Emotional Stress and Strain

You learned in Chapter 3 that nervous tension can cause headache. It can also cause constipation—or diarrhea. Whenever you become nervous, angry, or overly tense, distress signals spill over from your brain into the nerve pathways leading to your stomach and intestines. This can cause all sorts of digestive disturbances—and even disease.

It's especially important that you eliminate stress and tension at the dinner table. Turn back to Chapter 2 and study the recommendations for relieving nervous tensions.

9. If You Need an Enema

If your bowels fail to move after three or four days, it's much better to take an enema than to take a laxative that may cause spasm of the intestines. (You should *never* take a laxative when you have abdominal pain.) Water, the "universal solvent," will loosen the hardened and lumpy waste matter in your rectum and colon so that your stool may pass unobstructed. Chances are your bowels will then empty normally and regularly if you follow the recommendations outlined in this chapter.

COMPOSITION OF ENEMA: For a cleansing enema to soften and empty the lower bowel, mix two teaspoons of salt to one quart of warm water. Plain water is all right. Soap suds and other household "lubricants" may irritate the lining of the colon and rectum.

TECHNIQUE OF ENEMA: Lubricate the enema tip with KY Jelly, Vaseline, or baby oil and then insert it two to four inches into the rectum. The container holding the solution should be suspended 12 to 18 inches above the buttocks so that the liquid will flow into the rectum when the enema tube is unclamped.

The solution should flow slowly over a period of several minutes so that it won't be expelled prematurely by cramps. If cramps do occur, clamp the tube and wait a few seconds before continuing. A little pressure against the anus with a towel will prevent expulsion of the solution.

If possible, the quart of solution should be retained in the colon for five to ten minutes so that there is ample time for the water to soften the hardened waste matter.

The enema may be taken while lying on one side with the uppermost thigh and leg flexed or while in a knee-chest position. The latter position is probably best for retaining a large volume of water.

Uses of Oil

Persons who haven't had a bowel movement for a long time, and who may have a hard, impacted colon, can soften the contents of the colon by depositing three to six ounces of olive oil, cotton seed oil, or mineral oil in the rectum several hours before an enema or an attempted bowel movement.

Hard masses that present themselves at the anus may be broken up by inserting a finger into the rectum.

MINERAL OIL LAXATIVE: Since mineral oil is indigestible, it may be taken orally so that its passage through the intestine will enable it to infiltrate the entire length of the colon. Such oil shouldn't be taken very often, however, since it tends to wash certain oil-soluble vitamins right out of the intestinal tract. Unfortunately, there is a tendency for the oil to "leak" from the rectum before a bowel movement occurs.

The Dangers of Colonics

Be cautious about taking colonic irrigations. We now know that the large colon completes work left undone by the small intestine. Excessive flooding of the colon with water that flows in and out of the colon under pressure may wash away its mucous membrane and leave the walls of the colon inflamed and spastic. An enema may be just as effective for relieving constipation—and it's much safer.

10. A Posture for Relieving Gas Pains

Persons who suffer from constipation may also suffer from "gas pains" caused by an accumulation of gas in the portion of the colon just beneath the diaphragm. The best way to empty this pocket of gas is to get into a knee-chest position with the body weight supported on the knees and forearms. This will permit the gas to rise toward the buttocks so that it can be expelled.

Intestinal gas, also called "flatulence," is lighter than air. When there is an excessive amount of this gas in the colon, it tends to rise toward the diaphragm rather than follow the solid waste matter down into the lower colon. Whenever the knee-chest position is assumed, however, so that the buttocks are higher than the chest, the gas moves into the rectum.

If you're troubled with cramps caused by flatulence, try to assume the knee-chest position for a few minutes several times a day, especially before attending lengthy business or social functions. Elimination of gas may also stimulate bowel movement by loosening the contents of the colon.

Eliminate Gas-Forming Foods

You should, of course, try to eliminate foods that do not "agree" with you. Green salads, beans, cucumbers, and onions, for example, commonly cause flatulence. Different foods affect people differently, however. Some persons may find that milk is a gas former, while others may be disturbed by sweets.

If you suffer from gas pains, don't drink milk or eat green salads except with your evening meals. One patient who complained of cramping gas pains every afternoon was able to relieve her distress by drinking orange juice instead of milk each morning. Any gas-forming food eaten in the morning or at noon may cause distress before the end of the day.

Overeating or failure to chew your food adequately can also cause flatulence. Whenever you have to attend a function that you know will make you very nervous, eat simple carbohydrate foods that can be easily digested. Greasy foods or chunks of meat and vegetables in a nervous stomach can cause severe stomach cramps with excessive amounts of gas.

FOODS CONTAINING DIGESTIVE ENZYMES: If you think milk gives you gas pains, try eating a little yogurt each day. The bacteria in this nourishing food may prevent gas by aiding digestion.

Many persons suffer from gas because of improper digestion of protein. Papaya fruit and pineapple both contain protein-digesting enzymes that will aid digestion. Try to add these fruits to your diet whether you suffer from indigestion or not.

Relieving Gas Pains with Hot Packs

Cramps and gas pains in simple constipation or indigestion can sometimes be relieved by applying hot packs to the abdomen. You should be careful, however, not to put heat over an inflamed or infected appendix. If abdominal pain is accompanied by fever and other symptoms, see your doctor and follow his instructions.

Other Causes of "Gas"

There are many causes of flatulence. If your distress is not relieved by eliminating gas-forming foods and by observing the rules of good bowel care, see your doctor for a checkup. A "bad gall bladder," for example, is not an uncommon cause of excessive intestinal gas.

Try Sitting in a Sitz Bath

A sitz bath is sometimes helpful in the treatment of constipation and other types of pelvic trouble. Sit in a washtub or similar vessel full of cold water (45 to 60 degrees Fahrenheit) for five to ten minutes. (The stimulating effects of the cold water may also boost waning sexual powers.)

If a cold bath doesn't seem to help, try a hot sitz bath. Fill the vessel with hot water (110 degrees Fahrenheit) and sit in it for 15 to 20 minutes once or twice daily.

If neither the cold water nor the hot water seems to do the trick, try alternating them. Get *two* tubs and sit first in the hot water and then in the cold water. The circulatory stimulation of a contrast sitz bath has many benefits to offer the pelvic region. It is especially effective for persons suffering from chronic constipation.

PEPPERMINT FOR GASTRIC DISTRESS

Persons who use herbs claim that oil or essence of peppermint, taken orally, will relieve intestinal distress. For diarrhea, drink a solution of 15 drops of essence of peppermint in a cup of hot water. To relieve gas pains, put one drop of oil of peppermint in a cup of hot water, and drink that.

SUMMARY

1. Don't panic if you don't have a bowel movement every day. No real harm will result if you miss a couple of days. If you follow the recommendations outlined in this chapter, your bowels will function normally.

2. Each day, eat fruits and vegetables containing cellulose and other indigestible residue. Always eat the edible pulps and skins of fruits and vegetables.

3. Drink several glasses of water every day, or an equivalent amount of fruit and vegetable juices. When you get out of bed in the morning, drink a small glass of warm water that has been flavored by the juice of a section of lemon.

4. Make a special effort to eat your meals at the same time every day.

5. Never ignore an urge to empty your bowels. Try to visit the toilet on a regular schedule. Make sure that you allow adequate time for a complete and unhurried movement.

6. Include such trunk-bending exercises as sit-ups and bent-knee leg raises in a daily exercise program. If you don't want to exercise before breakfast, try to do so just before your evening meal.

7. If your bowels fail to move as usual, increase your intake of water and include bran-rich cereals and muffins in your diet.

8. You can encourage movement of your bowels by massaging the colon in its course up and around the abdomen from right to left.

9. If constipation is unrelieved after three or four days, and there is impaction of waste matter in your rectum, take a simple warm-water enema. Don't take a laxative unless your doctor prescribes one.

10. Constipation associated with abdominal pain or cramps requires special care that must be carried out under competent supervision.

5

Prevent Overweight and Hardening of the Arteries

Heart disease is the Nation's No. 1 killer. *After age 35, one death in every three is caused by disease of the heart and its blood vessels.* In practically all of these deaths, hard and clogged arteries account for the failure of the heart.

Unfortunately, hardening of the arteries is becoming increasingly more evident in young people. Autopsies performed on a number of young American soldiers killed in recent combat revealed that most of them were already showing evidence of arteriosclerosis. We were all shocked by recent headlines telling us that a small boy had died of "old man's arteries."

It has been increasingly evident that the American way of life—the food we eat, the tensions we suffer, and our reluctance to exercise—has a great deal to do with the spiraling death rate from heart disease. It should come as no surprise to learn that the more sedentary and overweight you are, the greater the chances that you have a weak heart that's supplied by hardened arteries.

You don't have to be fat and inactive to die from heart disease, however. Excessive smoking, unrelieved tension, improperly prepared foods, too much hard fat, artificial foods, and many other by-products of civilization can abuse your heart to death. Heart transplants notwithstanding, you have only one heart. It deserves the best care you can give it. If you want to live a long time, you should learn all you can about building a healthy heart—and you can begin by learning how to keep your arteries youthful and flexible.

AN EYE TEST FOR ARTERIAL DISEASE

If you're under 45 years of age, there is a simple way to tell if you're already a candidate for heart disease caused by hard, fat-ridden arteries. If there is a white or grayish ring (arcus senilis) around the edge of your iris, this may mean that there is far too much cholesterol or hard fat in your blood. (See Figure 5-1.)

Figure 5-1. A white ring just inside the colored portion of the eye (iris) may be a sign of excess blood fat.

The telltale fatty ring is actually in the cornea of the eye. But since the cornea is made up of transparent tissue that covers the iris (the portion of the eye containing the color), the ring appears to circle just inside the border of the iris. It is not uncommonly seen in elderly persons.

This chapter will tell you everything you need to know to prevent a build-up of fat in your arteries. Chapter 6 will tell you how to strengthen your heart. Don't wait until you're already up to your eyeballs in fat to begin a sensible diet. Once the fatty rings appear in your eyes, your life is already in danger.

THE FEMALE AND HARDENED ARTERIES

You already know that there are many causes of heart disease and hardened arteries. Some you can control and some you cannot. There are also some inherent factors that tend to *prevent* hardening of the arteries in some people. If you are a woman, for example, your sex is in your favor. Medical scientists have discovered that the symptoms of hardened arteries generally show up 10 to 20 years later in women than in men. This is believed to be due to female hormones that delay the onset of arterioscelerosis (also called "artherosclerosis").

As you grow older, a certain amount of arteriosclerosis cannot be avoided. You may even inherit a predisposition to arterial disease. You can't change your age, your sex, or your genes, but you can do something about some of the more common and controllable factors that are known to contribute to the development of cardiovascular disease.

HOW ONE MAN RECOVERED FROM A HEART ATTACK

Bill C., an attorney, was only 45, but he had already suffered a slight heart attack. His doctor told him that he was overweight and that he had too much fat (cholesterol) in his blood. After appropriate rest and medication, the doctor recommended many of the measures outlined in this chapter and in Chapter 6.

After several months of faithful adherence to the program, Bill C. was fit and trim. His blood cholesterol was back to normal and he no longer had chest pains when he exerted himself. Now, instead of exercising only occasionally, he was swimming and playing handball several times a week and enjoying every minute of it. Even though he was on a diet, he was never overly hungry. When he reached 50, he looked younger and healthier than he did at 40—and he felt better. He was sold on his new way of life. "I never intend to give up my diet and exercise program," he said.

You can follow the same program, and it can do as much for you as it did for this attorney.

Once you have suffered a heart attack, you should, of course, place yourself under the care of a physician, and you should submit to regular medical examinations. But anyone can follow the simple dietary recommendations outlined in this chapter.

THE FUNDAMENTALS OF DIET

In dieting for your heart's sake, there are two important effects to aim for: (1) keeping your body lean and (2) preventing a build-up of fat in your arteries and your blood.

Medical science doesn't know much about what causes hardening of the arteries, but there are a few theories, the most important of which are concerned with diet.

How Fat Overworks Your Heart

Too much fat on the body can overload a diseased heart by forcing it to pump blood through miles and miles of tiny blood vessels in the surplus fatty tissue. Too much fat in the blood can clog and harden important arteries to precipitate a serious or fatal coronary occlusion (heart attack).

Whenever the walls of the arteries are infiltrated and hardened by fat, the heart muscle and other tissues of the body may be deprived of adequate blood supply. If a clump of fat breaks loose from the wall of an artery anywhere in the body it may be carried along in the blood stream until it lodges in an artery around the heart. When this happens, a portion of the heart muscle may die and be replaced by scar tissue—if death does not occur. (See Figure 5-2.)

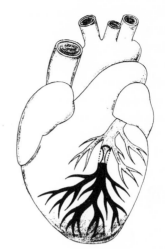

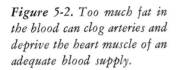

Figure 5-2. Too much fat in the blood can clog arteries and deprive the heart muscle of an adequate blood supply.

You Don't Have to Starve Yourself

Keeping your body and your arteries lean and healthy requires sensible day-to-day eating habits. If you eat properly and choose your foods carefully, you won't have to starve yourself or worry about eating too much. You can, in fact, literally gorge yourself on certain nonfattening foods. It's simply a matter of eating more of some foods and less of others.

An increased intake of fat-free protein foods will help prevent overweight by stimulating body metabolism. The more weight you lose and the leaner you become, the less you'll want to eat. It's now an established fact that excess weight (and an overstretched stomach) caused by unwise eating will falsely stimulate the appetite. Once you cut down on your eating and lose a few pounds, you won't be so hungry.

Overweight Americans spend a great deal of money on reducing remedies. There are even a few "reducing specialists" who routinely dispense "reducing pills" that are known to have harmful effects on the heart. The money squandered on these schemes could be spent much more wisely on wholesome, natural foods. Proper eating—and less eating—is the best way to reduce.

DON'T FORGET TO EXERCISE

Exercise is also very important in keeping lean for your heart's sake. In addition to burning off excess body weight, the right kind of exercise will also strengthen your heart muscle. Best of all, if you exercise regularly, you can eat a great deal more than you could otherwise.

There are some nutrition authorities who maintain that lack of exercise rather than overeating is the biggest cause of overweight in the United States.

We now know that exercise governs metabolism to help prevent a build-up of fat stores, even when the exercise burns fewer calories than contained in the individual's diet. This doesn't mean that you can continue eating large amounts of fattening foods, but it does mean that if you take exercise you can take in a proportionately greater number of calories without gaining weight.

Be sure to read Chapter 6 for additional information on how to reduce your body weight with the type of exercise that strengthens your heart.

DIETING TO KEEP A LEAN BODY

All overweight persons should first make an effort to reduce by cutting down on fat and carbohydrate foods. Carbohydrates are the chief fattening food in America. Most overweight persons who simply cut out bread and flour products, for example, would be able to lose weight. Sugar is also a carbohydrate; and in the average person's diet, it almost always represents excess calories.

Fortunately, the natural carbohydrate in such fruits and vegetables as bananas and potatoes is not nearly as fattening as refined carbohydrates.

Everyone, overweight or not, should reduce the amount of fat in the diet to a minimum. And there are certain types of fat, because of their effect on the heart and arteries, that should be eliminated altogether. You'll learn in other portions of this chapter that these fats, along with sugar, are a leading cause of hardening of the arteries.

A Good All-Around Diet

If you're not overweight and you're under 40 years of age, your daily diet should be made up of fruits, vegetables, milk, cheese, butter, meat (or poultry or fish), eggs, whole wheat bread, and whole grain cereals. See Chapter 12 for additional information on how to eat sensibly for good health.

Foods to Eliminate

If you're overweight, you should eliminate these foods from your diet: rich soups and gravies, fried foods, creamed foods, cream cheese, bread of all kinds, macaroni and spaghetti, grains and their products (flour, cereals, etc.), fats and oils, butter, candy, and all refined foods and beverages containing sugar, starch, or fat.

Foods That Aren't Fattening

You may eat generous amounts of these foods without fear of gaining weight: fresh fruits (except avocados), vegetables, green salads (without dressing), skim milk, cottage cheese, lean meat, fish, poultry, and eggs. All of these foods should, of course, be prepared without grease or oil.

You can satisfy your "sweet tooth" very quickly with dried fruits. Most dried fruits, like nuts, have a pretty high calorie content; but since they are natural foods, they usually satisfy the appetite without contributing excess calories. The same is true of such fruits and vegetables as bananas and potatoes.

If you're not greatly overweight, you can probably reduce simply by reducing the amount of food you eat, even if you don't eliminate some fattening foods altogether. Just eat smaller servings. Never eat until you are "full." Always quit eating when your "belt" begins to get tight. If you'll observe these simple rules, along with a little regular exercise, you won't have to worry about getting fat.

DIETING TO KEEP THE FAT OUT OF YOUR ARTERIES

As you grow older (over 40), you should make a special effort to reduce the amount of fat in your diet in order to protect your arteries. This will require observation of certain special rules.

Although it's still just a theory, many doctors believe that eating a certain kind of fat will contribute to hardening of the arteries in increasing the amount of cholesterol in the blood stream.

Animal Fat as a Source of Cholesterol

There is considerable evidence to indicate that excessive use of sugar and other carbohydrate foods will cause hardening of the arteries by forming fatty substances called "triglycerides." (The average American eats 100 pounds of sugar each year!) The consensus at the present time, however, is that *animal fat and dairy products are the two greatest sources of excess blood cholesterol.* This means that after middle age you should cut down on these foods, even if you aren't overweight.

Younger people who get plenty of physical exercise seem to be able to eat almost anything without an increase in blood cholesterol. But as you grow older and more inactive, the ability of your body to manufacture cholesterol from the basic food substances makes it necessary to cut down drastically on fatty and greasy foods.

Fats that remain hard or solid at room temperature are especially harmful. This type of fat is called "saturated fat," and it tends to harden in the blood vessels just as it does in a grease can. Unsaturated fat, on the other hand, does not harden, even when cooled, and it remains soft and liquid in the body.

Since animal fat is "hard" and vegetable fat is "soft," there are good reasons why you should decrease one and increase the other.

Vegetable Fat Reduces Blood Cholesterol

Liquid vegetable oils, such as corn oil, peanut oil, wheat germ oil, safflower oil, soybean oil, cottonseed oil, and sunflower oil, contain more unsaturated fat than saturated fat, which means that they tend to *reduce* hard fat in the blood rather than increase it. It seems that the unsaturated fatty acids act as a sort of detergent to prevent saturated fats from hardening.

Some health-minded persons ingest a couple of tablespoons of pure, cold-pressed (unheated) vegetable oil each day in order to balance the diet with unsaturated fat. Whenever the diet is high in linoleic acid, a soft fat found abundantly in corn oil, much of the dietary cholesterol is disposed of through the bowels.

You should always try to use liquid vegetable oils (except coconut oil and olive oil) rather than animal fat in your cooking. In addition to breaking down solid fat, vegetable oil is so easy for the body to burn that it won't contribute to overweight unless you're overeating generally.

Why You Shouldn't Cook with Solid Fats

You already know why you shouldn't use lard and other forms of animal fat in your cooking. A similar warning may be sounded about plain margarine. Whenever vegetable oils have been made hard by a process called "hydrogenation," they are usually higher in saturated fat. Lecithin, a fat-like substance that counteracts cholesterol, is also destroyed. There are, however, some recently developed solid vegetable fats that have been specially treated to retain lecithin as well as unsaturated fatty acids. Some margarines made with safflower oil, for example, claim to have more unsaturated fat than saturated fat.

It's important to remember, however, that all hard vegetable fats are treated with chemicals, which may make them less healthful than natural liquid fats. As a general rule, all hard fats contain a high percentage of saturated fat.

DANGERS OF COOKING WITH BACON GREASE: For obvious reasons, you should never use leftover bacon grease in cooking. In addition to being high in saturated fat, such previously heated animal fat may also contain decomposed and poisonous fatty acids (See Chapter 12). The practice of flavoring cooked vegetables with bacon grease is a bad one and should be discontinued.

THE IMPORTANCE OF INCLUDING SOME FAT IN THE DIET

Although fat should be reduced in everyone's diet, it should never be completely eliminated. A certain amount of fat is needed to supply certain essential fatty acids and to aid in the metabolism of carbohydrate. Without the unsaturated fatty acids, the cholesterol normally found in the blood would solidify and stick to the walls of your arteries, or form stones in your gall bladder.

Unfortunately, the average American's diet contains more than 40 percent fat. This should be reduced to 30 percent or less, depending upon your body weight. And whenever possible, vegetable fat should be substituted for animal fat so that animal fat does not make up more than half of the total fat intake. This would balance saturated and unsaturated fat to prevent a build-up of hard fat. Actually, for every gram of saturated fat in the diet, there should be two or three grams of unsaturated fat.

ALL MEAT CONTAINS FAT: It's practically impossible to eliminate all fat from the diet. Even lean meat may contain as much as 40 percent fat. So you don't have to worry about depriving your body of essential fatty acids if you eat some kind of meat each day.

Fish and Poultry Are Low in Saturated Fat

If you're concerned about blood cholesterol and hardened arteries, you should try to eat fish and poultry rather than beef and pork. Both fish and poultry contain less hard or saturated fat than other types of meat, and they contain proportionately more soft or unsaturated fat. They're also less expensive and just as tasty, and they're just as rich in protein.

INCREASE YOUR PROTEIN INTAKE

Regardless of the type of diet you're on, you should not attempt to reduce your protein intake, since this could result in muscular weakness and other symptoms. There is some evidence to indicate that a high-protein diet is a deterrent to heart disease. Doctors who made a study of 100,000 members of the Masai tribe of East Africa found that they had an extremely low level of blood cholesterol and that heart attacks caused by clogging of the coronary arteries were rare. Their diet consists mainly of meat, blood, and sour milk. (Also, members of the Masai walk many miles each day.)

FAT-FREE MEAT SUBSTITUTES: If you must eliminate all meat from your diet for some reason (on doctor's orders only!), you can get your protein from egg white, skim milk, cottage cheese, and yogurt. These foods are completely free from all forms of fat. You can make a fat-free, high-protein drink by mixing powdered skim milk with regular skim milk.

Nuts and soy beans are rich in protein as well as unsaturated fatty acids.

OTHER DIETARY FACTORS TO BE CONSIDERED IN PREVENTING HARDENED ARTERIES

There's more to preventing arteriosclerosis than simply eliminating hard fat. An increased intake of certain foods along with vegetable oil might be beneficial.

The Role of Apple Pectin

Some researchers have found that a substance called "fruit pectin," found abundantly in the meat or pomace of apples, tends to lower blood pressure and combat hardening of the arteries. The individual who first said that "an apple a day keeps the doctor away" was on the right track after all. (Apples also clean the teeth! When it's not possible to brush your teeth after eating, try to conclude your meal by eating an apple, a carrot, or a piece of celery.) Pectin is also found in the inner portion of the rind of citrus fruits. So don't worry too much about peeling off all that white substance that separates the meat of the orange from its rind.

The skins and rinds of most fruits and vegetables undoubtedly contain healthful food substances. Try to eat them whenever they prove to be tasty as well as edible. Always eat the pulp of oranges and other juice fruits. This will provide pectin as well as roughage for your bowels.

Supplement Your Diet with Lecithin

Lecithin, a phospholipid found in egg yolk, grains, meat, and in some vegetables and cereals, as well as in natural animal and vegetable fats, prevents precipitation of cholesterol by breaking up blood fat into tiny globules. Whenever these foods are cooked or processed, however, the lecithin is destroyed. Since most of us prefer to cook our meat and eggs, it might be a good idea to supplement the diet with lecithin tablets in order to counteract the remaining cholesterol.

Always trim the fat from cooked meat. Any kind of heated animal fat is a potent source of cholesterol, with no lecithin to hold it in check.

Soy beans and cold-pressed soy bean oil are rich in lecithin. Avocados are a good source of lecithin and unsaturated fatty acids.

The Fat-Dissolving B Vitamins

Certain B vitamins—choline, inositol, and pyridoxine—also play an important part in preventing hardening of the arteries by dispersing globules of fat in much the same way that lecithin does. See Chapter 12 for good sources of Vitamin B.

The Benefits of Garlic

Many people (and some doctors) maintain that garlic tends to lower blood pressure as well as prevent hardening of the arteries. It is definitely a nutritious herb that may have many beneficial effects in the body. If you don't like the odor that remains in your mouth after chewing garlic, you can buy garlic tablets that may be swallowed whole.

Go Easy on Salt!

Too much salt in the diet tends to harden the arteries and raise blood pressure. If you work hard and perspire a lot, you need more salt than the average person, and you may even have to take salt tablets. But if you live the average sedentary life, don't oversalt the foods you eat. Remember that most foods already contain a little natural salt in their mineral content. Too much salt will force your body to retain too much water in your tissues— and this can be harmful.

If you have high blood pressure, your doctor may ask you to eliminate table salt altogether.

Tension as a Source of Cholesterol

Although diet is probably the biggest source of excess blood cholesterol, it's well known that the body manufactures the cholesterol it needs to nourish the nervous system and insulate nerves. It's equally well known that simple nervous tension can raise blood cholesterol to a dangerously high level, even when the patient is on a low-fat diet. For this reason, many doctors routinely prescribe lecithin granules for all their patients who show a high blood fat.

You can eliminate much of your nervous tension if you practice the relaxing techniques outlined in Chapter 2.

SUMMARY

If you're somewhat confused about dieting for your heart's sake, remember these important points:

1. Try to eat more fish and poultry than beef or pork. Trim all fat from the meats you eat. Don't eat such fat-rich meats as bacon, sausage, corned beef, and animal organs.

2. Use liquid vegetable oils in your cooking, but avoid fried foods whenever possible. Don't eat any kind of solid fat.

3. Reduce your intake of dairy products (butter, cream, cheese, ice cream).

4. Replace cheese and butter with cottage cheese and margarine. Select margarine that has been specially treated to retain lecithin and unsaturated fatty acids.

5. Eliminate or cut down on pastries, cakes, cookies, and other desserts and sweets that have been prepared with refined sugar, animal fat, or hydrogenated vegetable fat.

6. Balance your diet with fruits, vegetables, whole grain cereals, pure whole wheat bread, and skim milk.

7. Don't eat more than one whole egg each day; if you do, remove the yolks. Egg yolk contains both lecithin and cholesterol, but the lecithin is destroyed by cooking.

8. Avoid rich, processed, or artificial foods. Try to eat fresh, natural foods —and eat them raw whenever possible.

9. If you have a high blood cholesterol, or if your diet is high in hard fat, supplement your diet with lecithin granules and a tablespoonful or two of cold-pressed vegetable oil.

10. Remember that a lean diet with regular exercise is the key to preventing premature hardening and clogging of the arteries.

6

Strengthen Your Heart for Longer Life and Better Health

The heart does a tremendous amount of work. Each day, it pumps the equivalent of 5,500 quarts of blood through more than 60,000 miles of blood vessels. Whenever you get out and run, however, your heart must pump up to six gallons of blood per minute to supply your muscles with adequate oxygen.

What a miraculous thing it is that the hollow muscle we call a "heart" can sustain life with round-the-clock pumping action. Although the heart pumps involuntarily as an organ, it must be given special attention as a muscle if it is to hold up under unrelenting stress.

What you learn in this chapter will enable you to build a heart that won't "break down" prematurely. Old age will eventually catch up with us all. But if you take good care of your heart, it can outlast the rest of your body. Properly nourished and conditioned, the heart is probably the toughest organ in the body.

EXERCISE WON'T STRAIN A NORMAL HEART

People used to believe that exercise was bad for the heart. They thought that any unnecessary work placed on the heart would simply "wear it out," since it was already working quite hard in pumping blood through the body. Most doctors recommended rest rather than exercise, "just to be safe."

Today, we know that heart muscle is similar to the muscle in our biceps, and that exercise makes it *stronger* rather than weaker. When a heart is required to do more than pump blood through an inactive body, it becomes just as weak as the body. In other words, when you condition your body you condition your heart.

IMPORTANCE OF HAVING YOUR HEART EXAMINED

It is important, of course, to make sure that your heart is normal before you begin an exercise program. Although strenuous exercise won't ordinarily damage a healthy heart, a diseased heart might not be able to withstand certain types of exercise.

If you do have heart trouble, or if you have ever had a heart attack, your doctor might be able to prescribe special supervised exercises that will strengthen your heart muscle and flush out your coronary arteries.

THE KEY: INCREASING HEART RATE AND RESPIRATION

Any kind of exercise that makes you breathe heavily and your heart beat faster will strengthen your heart. But you must *begin lightly and then exercise regularly and progressively over a long period of time.* You simply increase the amount of exercise you do as your heart becomes stronger.

Running, swimming, and riding a bicycle are excellent forms of exercise. The large amount of blood that the heart must pump through the muscles of the thighs and legs will increase both the strength and the efficiency of the heart. As the muscle fibers in the heart become thicker and more dense, a slower heart rate will pump out a greater volume of blood. (See Figure 6-1.)

Figure 6-1. Bicycle riding is an entertaining form of exercise that will burn fat and improve circulation.

WIDENING THE HEART ARTERIES WITH EXERCISE

The increased flow of blood through the coronary arteries in endurance-type exercise will increase the size and flexibility of the all-important coronary arteries. This will improve the blood supply to the heart muscle itself and lessen chances of one of the arteries being clogged by a clot or a glob of fat. Tiny new arteries and capillaries will also open throughout the heart muscle, giving the heart a reserve blood supply if one of the larger arteries is ever closed by a "coronary occlusion."

EXERCISE REDUCES BLOOD FAT

There is considerable evidence to indicate that endurance-type exercise involving use of the legs will reduce the amount of fat in the blood. Research at the Valley Forge Heart Institute, for example, revealed that the cholesterol and triglyceride levels of marathon runners were considerably lower than those of the average man. In runners over 35 years of age, there was a "dramatic absence" of hardening of the arteries.

One man whose blood serum cholesterol was at a dangerous 230 index reduced it to a "safe" 200 index by eliminating animal fat from his diet (see Chapter 5) and by riding his bicycle to and from work each day.

Try to Exercise Every Other Day

In order for any exercise to be effective, it should be performed at least twice a week—preferably every other day. Once a week is not often enough to become accustomed to the exercise, and it won't burn enough calories or have enough effect on your body metabolism to keep your body lean. The heart, like any other muscle of the body, must be conditioned by regular and frequent exercise to gain in strength and endurance. Strenuous exercise only once or twice a month will do more harm than good.

REDUCE YOUR BODY WEIGHT WHILE YOU
STRENGTHEN YOUR HEART

If you're considerably overweight, you should try to exercise daily until your body weight drops to a desirable level. You don't have to run 20 miles or drive yourself to the point of exhaustion. Just exercise until you are comfortably fatigued. After several weeks, you'll find that you can exercise for a much longer period of time before fatigue compels you to stop.

Fifteen or 20 minutes of endurance-type exercise two or three times a week won't condition your body for athletic competition, but it will keep your heart strong enough to withstand stress.

RUNNING IS THE BEST EXERCISE

Simple running or jogging is probably the best and most convenient form of exercise for the heart. The oxygen debt created in the big muscles of the thighs will force the heart to pump more blood than any other form of exercise. Also, the alternate contraction and relaxation of the thigh muscles will act as a subsidiary pump to aid the heart in moving a large volume of blood (see Chapter 13). (See Figure 6-2.)

Figure 6-2. Outdoor jogging is the best exercise for strengthening the heart and lungs.

Walking is a fairly good exercise, but it doesn't create enough of an oxygen debt to really exercise the heart muscle. ("Running in place" is a good indoor exercise but it's hard on the ankles and the lower back.)

REMEMBER: If an exercise doesn't make you breathe heavily, it's not doing much for your heart.

Begin Lightly and Progressively

Begin your running exercise by alternately walking and jogging around the block; that is, walk for awhile and then jog for awhile. Don't push yourself too hard. As you become better conditioned, you can jog more and walk less—until you can jog around the block nonstop.

Once you become accustomed to jogging, you can give your heart extra exercise by running a little faster. If you run a mile each day, for example, you should strive to cover the distance in as short a period of time as possible. Why jog 20 miles if you can exercise your heart just as well by running two miles?

THE CASE OF THE ATHLETIC RATS

In experiments with rats, Dr. Hans Selye, one of the world's leading authorities on stress, found that rats that were forced to exercise regularly would later survive stresses that resulted in heart failure in sedentary rats.

Don't be a sedentary person. You never know when you may be forced to call upon your heart for support in a physical emergency. Everyone needs a little extra heart strength to run after a bus occasionally or to take full advantage of infrequent holiday outings. What if your boat turns over and you have to swim a couple of miles to reach shore?

If you're healthy but underexercised, it's not likely that your heart will fail before your body will when you exert yourself. But if you're prone to collapse from sheer fatigue in prolonged unaccustomed exertion, you may not be able to save yourself—or someone else—if an emergency does arise.

CHECK YOUR HEART WITH THESE SIMPLE PULSE-RATE TESTS

Before you begin your jogging exercise, try these simple pulse-rate tests to see if your heart muscle is lagging behind your skeletal muscles. After several weeks of exercise, repeat the tests to see if an improvement occurs.

TEST 1: Take your resting pulse rate for one minute while sitting in a chair. You can do this by placing the fingers of your right hand over the thumbside of the inside portion of your left wrist. (The average pulse rate is about 72. But the more fit you are, the slower your pulse will be.) Record the pulse count on a piece of paper so that you can refer to it later.

Next, run "in place" for about five minutes or until you are "out of breath." Then sit in a chair and take your pulse again after one minute of rest. If it exceeds 110, you're in poor physical condition.

You should no longer be breathless after two minutes of rest. After ten minutes, your pulse should be back to normal.

TEST 2:   On a different day, when you haven't been exercising, take your pulse rate while standing up and while lying down. The closer together these two readings are, the more adaptable your heart is to the stresses placed upon it. If the two readings are wide apart, you should make a special effort to strengthen your heart with endurance-type exercise.

OTHER FORMS OF EXERCISE

If you don't want to run, try swimming in the summer and riding a bicycle in the winter. Keep a jumping rope handy so that you can exercise indoors when the weather is too bad to go outdoors.

You can make a good jumping rope by taping handles to each end of a long piece of window sash cord. The rope should be just long enough to hit the floor and clear the top of your head when it is swung from the belt line.

How to Jump a Rope

Jumping a rope properly requires practice and skill. If you've ever watched a school girl jump rope, you know that she jumps, skips, and jumps; that is, she jumps twice for each revolution of the rope. In order to get the most out of rope jumping, you should jump only *once* for each revolution of the rope, and you should lift both feet together. By jumping on your toes and limiting the jump to only a couple of inches, you can swing the rope much faster and jump much more rapidly. Your arms should be close to your body on each side so that a rotating wrist and forearm action can be used to swing the rope. With a little practice, you should be able to jump rope just like a boxer in a beautiful display of rope-jumping skill. (See Figure 6-3.)

WATCH FOR DANGER SIGNALS

One reason for beginning any kind of exercise slowly and progressively is to prevent disability from sore and lame muscles. But the most important reason is to prevent strain in the event there is an undiscovered heart disorder.

As you gradually increase the demands of your exercise, bring any unusual symptoms to the attention of your doctor. Agonizing breathlessness, a rapidly pounding or skipping heart, chest pain following exertion, inability to sleep or unusual restlessness following exercise, extreme weakness or shakiness that lasts for more than ten minutes after exercising, or fatigue that lasts longer than one day, for example, may point to possible heart disease. If such symptoms persist after several weeks of exercise, see a heart specialist for a complete checkup.

Figure 6-3. Rope jumping is a good exercise for both men and women.

EXERCISING YOUR BICEPS AND OTHER MUSCLES

If you want to develop the muscles of your body, you should include a little low-repetition resistance exercise. Weightlifting, for example, will greatly improve your physical appearance. Pushups, chins, and other body weight exercises will also enlarge the skeletal muscles. It's important to remember, however, that such exercise does very little for your heart. So while you should try to include some type of heavy resistance exercise in your training program, you should give priority to endurance-type exercise (high repetitions) in order to keep your body lean and your heart strong. (See Figure 6-4.)

The older you become, the more important it is to exercise regularly.

Figure 6-4. Weight training will improve physical appearance by develop-ing the skeletal muscles, but it does not do much for the heart.

HELPING YOUR HEART WITH BREATHING EXERCISES

Few people realize that breathing helps the heart circulate blood. The negative pressure that draws air into the lungs during an inspiration also has a suction effect on the big veins leading to the heart. This helps the blood circulation to overcome the pull of gravity in its uphill journey back to the heart.

Breathe deeply when you walk or exercise. Be sure to read Chapter 14 for descriptions of breathing exercises.

EMOTIONAL STRESS CAN STRAIN YOUR HEART

In Chapters 3 and 4, you learned that nervous tension can cause headache and constipation. It can also affect your heart. Constant harassment at home or on the job can bombard your heart and blood vessels with noxious nervous stimuli that can overwork your heart muscle and harden your arteries.

Nervous constriction of the arteries around the heart can even cause chest pain by depriving the heart muscle of adequate oxygen. Doctors call this pain "angina pectoris." It's very similar to the discomfort suffered by some sedentary persons whose coronary arteries are too small or too hard to supply the heart with adequate blood during unaccustomed exertion.

Turn back to Chapter 2 and review the instructions on how to relieve nervous tension. If you can learn to relax your muscles several times a day, you can relax your blood vessels as well as your nerves.

SMOKING AND YOUR HEART

There is a great deal of evidence to indicate that cigarette smoking contributes to death from heart disease. Nicotine deprives the heart of oxygen by speeding up the heart rate and constricting the blood vessels supplying the heart muscle. Whenever these effects are combined with hardened arteries, overweight, lack of exercise, and emotional stress, the results can be disastrous.

Nicotine can be absorbed into the blood stream through the mucous membrane of the mouth just as readily as through the lungs. So if you have heart disease, don't smoke, even if you don't inhale.

If you'd like to have additional information about the effects of cigarette smoking, alcohol drinking, and exercise on the heart, send to Parker Publishing Company (West Nyack, New York 10994) for a copy of my book *Muscle Training for Athletes.*

SUMMARY

1. Be sure to observe the rules in Chapter 5, along with the exercises described in this chapter, if you want to build a strong heart without arteries that have been hardened by an improper diet.

2. Any kind of exercise that increases heart rate and respiration will strengthen the heart muscle. An increase in the size of the normal heart from endurance-type exercise represents a healthy thickening of the muscle fibers of the heart.

3. Exercise won't strain a normal heart. But if you have heart trouble, you should exercise under the supervision of a physician.

4. Jogging, swimming, jumping a rope, and riding a bicycle will exercise your heart by forcing it to pump blood to the large muscles of the thighs.

5. Whatever type of exercise you do, you should begin lightly and then increase the training load slowly and progressively over a long period of time. Try to exercise at least twice a week, preferably every other day.

6. Take the pulse-rate tests (described in this chapter) to check on the condition and progress of your heart.

7. Regular exercise will lessen chances of a heart attack by widening the arteries that supply the heart muscle and by opening tiny new arteries and capillaries inside the heart.

8. Smoking places an extra load on your heart by stimulating the nervous system and constricting the blood vessels.

9. Unrelieved nervous tension raises your blood pressure, increases blood fat, overworks your heart, and constricts and hardens the coronary arteries.

7

Cope with Arthritis
Effectively and Painlessly

There are many types of arthritis; some are caused by infection, some by wear and tear, and some by emotional stress and strain. Whatever the cause, more than 12 million Americans suffer from this dreaded disease. Every day, at least 68,000 of them are absent from work because of pain or illness due to "arthritis and rheumatism."

Everyone is a potential victim of arthritis. There is, however, a great deal that can be done to prevent arthritis. There is also a great deal that an arthritic can do to help himself. If you've ever had a joint pain, you'll want to study this chapter carefully.

TYPES OF ARTHRITIS

If you already have arthritis, you should be examined by a physician in order to determine what type it is. There is no complete cure for some forms of arthritis, and medication may do nothing more than relieve the symptoms. But if you should happen to have gouty arthritis or an infectious arthritis, medication may be essential for relief of pain or to kill the infection. Also, any underlying organic disease—such as anemia—that may contribute to the development of joint disease should be properly treated.

GENERAL GUIDELINES IN CONTROLLING ARTHRITIS

Good posture, improved nutrition, avoiding overwork and physical strain, healthy bowels, relief from nervous tension and emotional stress and strain, and good living habits in general are all important in controlling arthritis.

Practically everything you'll learn in this book will be useful in combating arthritis. There are, however, some special recommendations for arthritics who want to remain fully active and productive as the years go by.

TWO COMMON FORMS OF ARTHRITIS

In the greatest majority of cases, arthritis will fall into one of two categories: rheumatoid arthritis or osteoarthritis.

Rheumatoid Arthritis: The Disease of "Young Folks"

Rheumatoid arthritis is the most serious, and it usually strikes before the individual reaches forty years of age. Because of the tendency of this disease to cripple some persons by permanently stiffening the affected joints, it's important that the victim remain under the care of a competent specialist.

Sometimes the disease will "burn out" before any serious crippling occurs. Too frequently, however, the affected joints become fused together before any relief from symptoms occurs.

WOMEN AFFECTED MORE OFTEN THAN MEN: For some reason not yet known to medical science, rheumatoid arthritis is three times more common among women than among men.

Osteoarthritis: The Disease of "Old Folks"

The most common—and fortunately the least serious—form of arthritis is called "osteoarthritis." It occurs primarily *after* forty years of age, and it's the result of injury and wear and tear on the joints. As the joint surfaces become rough and thick, movement becomes difficult and painful. (See Figure 7-1.)

Figure 7-1. In osteoarthritis, movement of an affected joint may be hindered by adhesions and bony spurs.

Everyone Will Eventually Suffer from Osteoarthritis

Practically everyone past middle age will have a certain amount of osteoarthritis. Some people are affected more than others. Most of the time, there is only a small amount of stiffness and soreness. Occasionally, however, the disease will cause painful disability that grows worse with age.

If you're now suffering from osteoarthritis, self help can be very important in improving your physical condition and in easing your discomfort. In fact, how well you get along in time to come will depend almost entirely upon *you!*

Take the case of Arthur L., for example. When he first began to develop symptoms of arthritis in his hands and knees, he told his wife, "Well, I guess I'm just getting old. Time to slow down a little."

Although Arthur was only 45, he used his arthritis as an excuse to "take it easy." He had heard that there was no cure for arthritis, so he didn't feel that it was necessary to see a doctor. After a couple of years of "resting," his joints were so stiff that he had difficulty getting dressed. By the time he reached 50, he was "older" than a 70-year-old man.

Joseph C. took a different course of action. He was given a self-help program that he could follow from day to day. He was never completely free from the symptoms of arthritis, but he did not become a cripple. He remained unusually active and aggressive for a 65-year-old man, and he continued to enjoy all the pleasures that life had to offer.

Whether you are a man or a woman, you can do as Joseph C. did and help yourself in overcoming the hindrance of arthritis. All you have to do is to follow the suggestions outlined in this chapter.

RELIEVING THE DISCOMFORTS OF ARTHRITIS

Even though there is no way to get rid of the bony growths that develop around the joints in osteoarthritis, such simple measures as rest, exercise, posture control, diet, massage, heat, and aspirin will relieve soreness and stiffness. Properly applied, these same measures can be used to prevent as well as relieve disability.

Balancing Rest and Exercise

It's important to keep arthritic joints moving in order to keep them from getting too stiff. This means that you should *move the affected joints through a full range of movement several times each day.*

Any kind of moderate exercise might be beneficial if it does not result in fatigue or pain. Too much exercise can be worse than none. You need just enough exercise to keep your muscles well toned and your joints flexible, but not so much that it increases the pain and soreness in your joints. This means that you should get a certain amount of exercise and a certain amount of rest. But you'll have to learn from experience how to balance your rest and exercise for best results.

A 68-year-old retired railroad man complained that he was so stiff when he got out of bed in the morning that he could hardly move. And the more he rested, the stiffer he became. He was able to relieve his stiffness, however, by taking a hot bath and then moving his joints about in simple calisthenics. He walked around the block twice a day and rested for an hour or so after each meal. Every Tuesday and Friday, he went swimming at the YMCA.

By exercising a little and resting a little, the "old railroad man" got along fine. "I feel much better than I did when I just sat around the house," he said.

Don't try to exercise arthritic joints by performing hard work! The main purpose of the exercise for arthritis is to keep the joints from becoming stiff, not to enlarge the muscles.

Special Exercises for "Frozen Joints"

If your joints are so sore and stiff that you cannot move them through a full range of movement, it will be necessary to use special exercises to loosen your joints. In particularly severe cases, the assistance of a therapist may be necessary. By gradually forcing an increased range of movement from day to day in a progressive exercise program, it may be possible to restore useful movement and prevent deformity with very little discomfort.

In some cases, manipulation must be used to break down adhesions that literally glue arthritic joints together. The spinal column, in particular, can benefit from an occasional joint-popping manipulation. Such treatment can be performed by a chiropractor, an osteopath, or a physiatrist.

It's much easier to prevent stiffness than to relieve it. Try to maintain your flexibility by moving your joints as far as you can each day.

Using Traction on Your Neck

If you have arthritis in your neck, you may be able to reduce stiffness and relieve symptoms by using the neck-stretching techniques described in Chapter 3.

Maintaining Erect Posture

Regardless of what type of arthritis you might have, it's very important to sit, stand, and sleep in positions that won't allow your joints to stiffen in a bent or deformed position. If you have arthritis in your spine, for example, you should keep your spine straight or erect at all times. If you slump over a desk or a work bench, you may one day discover that you cannot completely straighten up.

Too Much Sitting Can Be Bad

Improper sitting posture can do a great deal of harm to an arthritic spine. Too much sitting, even when you sit properly, is also bad for arthritic hips, knees, and elbows. The reason for this is that prolonged flexion of the joints may allow muscle shortening and joint adhesions to block extension of the joints. And if you ever allow your hip muscles to shorten in a sitting position, they'll exert such a pull on your spinal column that you'll begin to slump a little. When this happens, it's just a matter of time before the pull of gravity bends your spine into a bow.

Chapter 9 will tell you how to sit and stand correctly, how to make your bed firm for good sleeping posture, and how to stretch the muscles in your hips.

Alternate Sitting and Standing Postures

If your job requires a lot of sitting, you should, of course, maintain correct sitting posture at all times. But you should also make a special effort to stand erect many times during working hours so that you can completely straighten out your joints. Put both arms over your head, stand on your toes, and reach for the sky.

Don't Use a Pillow Under Arthritic Knees!

You'll learn in Chapter 9 that backache can sometimes be relieved by lying on your back with a pillow under both knees. If you have arthritis in your back, hips, or knees, however, you shouldn't use a pillow in this manner, since it may contribute to stiffening of the knees and the lower spine in a bent position.

Try to sleep with your body straight and your joints extended in a relaxed position. In other words, sleep flat on your back (on a firm mattress) with your arms at your sides.

Reduce Your Body Weight

The more overweight you are, the greater the strain on arthritic joints. If you observe the dietary and exercise recommendations outlined in Chapters 5 and 6, you won't have a weight problem.

Relieving Pain and Stiffness with Heat

If you have osteoarthritis, you know from experience that you can relieve soreness and stiffness by "warming up" with a little exercise. You can get even more benefit from your exercise if you apply a little moist heat to the affected joints beforehand. You should, in fact, apply heat to sore joints as frequently as you can, whether you exercise or not.

Methods of Applying Heat

Whenever your entire body is affected by arthritis, you should simply immerse your body in a tub of hot water (100 to 102 degrees Fahrenheit) for 15 to 20 minutes. But whenever isolated joints are affected, as in the hands, elbows, ankles, or spine, you'll get more benefit from local applications of heat. This can be accomplished by applying hot towels, heat lamps, hot water, or hot paraffin to the sore joint.

Hot Fomentations for Chronic Arthritis

Moist heat is undoubtedly the most effective form of heat for relieving chronic joint inflammation. This can be applied simply and effectively by wringing out strips of flannel in hot water and then placing them over the affected joint.

The flannel will retain the heat, while the cotton over it will retain the moisture. You can avoid blistering your skin by first covering the area to be treated with a dry cloth. Both the cloth and the moist flannel may then be covered by a sheet of oil cloth to hold in the heat.

It might be a good idea to wear rubber gloves when wringing out a hot, wet cloth—just to make sure that you don't blister your hands.

Using a Heating Pad

If you have a heating pad that's insulated by a rubber bag, you can keep moist towels hot by laying the pad over the towels. Otherwise you may apply moist flannel to your body and then cover this with a sheet of rubber or plastic before applying the heating pad.

Whatever you do, don't let the moisture in the cloth come into contact with the electrical wiring in the pad.

WARNING: You should never go to sleep while using a heating pad. Prolonged application of heat may dull the sensitivity of the skin enough to permit a bad burn without your being aware of it. Don't ever apply heat over a diseased or "dead" portion of the skin where sensation is impaired.

Using a Heat Lamp

Moist heat may also be applied by shining an infrared (heat) bulb onto a wet cloth. These lamps may be purchased in any drug store. They are *not* the same thing as a "sun lamp." Make sure that you get an *infrared* rather than an *ultraviolet* lamp. (See Figure 7-2.)

Figure 7-2. An infrared bulb, rather than an ultraviolet lamp, should be used to heat arthritic joints.

CAUTION: If you have diabetes, be careful not to burn yourself, since this could result in a slow-healing wound that may easily become infected. An ultraviolet lamp can blister the skin without any sensation of heat. Don't ever use such lamps for treatment purposes.

Benefits of a Paraffin Bath

If you have arthritis in your hands, you may simply immerse them in a pan of hot water for an immediate and effective form of moist heat.

For variety, however, you might want to try dipping your hands into hot paraffin. A 52-year-old cosmetics sales lady who tried this technique said that it relieved the soreness and stiffness in her fingers when nothing else seemed to help. The sealing, penetrating effect of hot wax has a potent heating effect on the circulation as well as the joints.

TECHNIQUE OF PARAFFIN BATH: Melt three pounds of ordinary paraffin in a three-quart double boiler and then stir in six ounces of mineral oil. Heat the mixture to a temperature of 125 degrees Fahrenheit.

If you don't have a bath thermometer to test the temperature of the melted paraffin, just remove it from the stove and let it cool until the surface begins to congeal before you use it.

Dip your hand into the paraffin mixture several times so that it will be coated with a thick glove of congealed paraffin. It will, of course, be necessary to pause a few seconds between dippings in order for each layer of paraffin to congeal. Let your fingers hang relaxed during the dipping. (See Figure 7-3.)

Figure 7-3. A paraffin bath provides an excellent heat treatment for arthritic hands and feet.

You can conserve the heat by wrapping your paraffin-coated hand with a piece of flannel. After 20 minutes or so, simply peel the paraffin from your hand and save it for the next treatment.

CAUTION: Since paraffin is inflammable, be careful not to spill any over an open flame.

If your hands are hairy, you might want to shave them to prevent any discomfort in removing the hardened wax.

Mustard Plasters for Arthritis Relief

If simple moist heat does not seem to relieve the symptoms of arthritis, you might want to try a mustard plaster. This is an old folk remedy that has withstood the test of time. The harmless skin irritation produced by mustard stimulates the nerves to release a histamine-like substance deep within the joints and tissues. This increases the blood circulation around arthritic joints by dilating tiny blood vessels.

Basically, a mustard plaster acts very much like liniments that relieve pain through a process called "counter-irritation." Simply rubbing a sore joint with a slice of garlic will sometimes relieve pain by irritating the skin and increasing the circulation.

HOW TO MAKE A MUSTARD PLASTER: Mix one part mustard with four to six parts flour (for adults only!) and then stir in just enough warm water to make a smooth paste. *Do not boil the mixture, and do not use hot water!* If the temperature of the water you use is over 140 degrees Fahrenheit, the oil of mustard will not be released and the plaster won't be effective.

Spread the mustard paste about one-quarter of an inch thick over a sheet of muslin that has been spread out in a bread pan that is being kept warm by the eye of a stove. Place another sheet of muslin over the top of the spread mixture. Fold the edges over to prevent leakage.

Be sure to cut the sheets of muslin to the right size beforehand so that they'll adequately cover the joints you want to treat.

After the plaster has been applied, lift it up and examine the skin every five minutes for redness. *When a definite pink color appears, remove the plaster.* If you leave the plaster on too long, you might blister the skin severely.

After you have removed the plaster, wash the skin with soap and water and then apply a little baby oil to prevent chapping.

Go Easy on Massage

Massage can be helpful in relaxing tight muscles and in increasing circulation, but it should not be used over an acutely painful joint. *Mechanical vi-*

brators or massage machines should never be applied over an arthritic joint. Such jarring may aggravate the disease by irritating the sensitive joint surfaces.

TECHNIQUE FOR MASSAGING AN ARTHRITIC JOINT: Apply a little oil to your skin. Then use a light finger-tip stroking over the joint, with a firm kneading of the muscles above and below the affected joint. Always rub towards the heart.

Massage is *not* a substitute for exercise or movement of the joints. All the massage in the world won't do as much to prevent joint stiffness as occasionally moving the joints through a full range of movement.

A SPECIAL EXERCISE FOR PERSONS WITH SPINAL ARTHRITIS

If you have spinal arthritis, you should make a special effort to keep your spine erect and your rib cage up. Once you begin to develop a hump or a roundness in your upper back, and your rib cage begins to flatten, you won't be able to assume an erect posture. Worst of all, the deformity will tend to worsen as you become older.

There is, however, a special exercise that you can do to keep your spine straight and your chest up. Try to do the exercise following other forms of exercise that make you breathe heavily.

The Straight-Arm Pullover from an Ottoman

Lie back over an ottoman (padded foot stool) so that your back is supported between your shoulders. Keep your knees bent and both feet flat on the floor. Hold a weight at arm's length over your chest. Lower the weight back over your head with straight arms, inhaling deeply as the weight goes back. (See Figure 7-4.)

You should use a very light weight in this exercise so that you can lift your chest up high as you inhale. The pressure of the ottoman against your back will straighten and adjust your spine, while forced expansion of your lungs will stretch your rib cage. Do several repetitions at least every other day.

If you have a barbell, try using about five pounds on each end of the bar. You can make a barbell by securing a ten-pound bag of sand to each end of a broomstick. Or you may simply use a single bag of sand that weighs about 15 pounds. In any event, make sure that the weight is light enough to permit at least four very easy repetitions.

Figure 7-4. Straight-arm pullovers from an ottoman will keep an arthritic spine straight.

USING EXERCISE TO RELIEVE PAIN: A 38-year-old postal clerk who had to stand long hours sorting mail complained of "pain and pressure" in the portion of his spine between his shoulder blades. He took an ottoman and a bag of sand to the post office and did straight-arm pullovers two or three times during working hours. He reported complete relief from pain and a diminishing of fatigue at the end of the day.

ASPIRIN: THE "WONDER DRUG" FOR ARTHRITIS

In particularly severe forms of arthritis in which simple physical therapy does not afford adequate relief from pain, aspirin may be used to relieve symptoms and reduce inflammation. In fact, aspirin is more effective in the treatment of arthritis than any of the more expensive and high-powered drugs—and it's much safer.

This doesn't mean, however, that you should discontinue use of all the self-help techniques outlined in this chapter. Even if you do find it necessary to take aspirin occasionally, you should continue to make a special effort to keep your muscles toned and your joints loose.

DON'T TAKE TOO MUCH ASPIRIN: Like most drugs, aspirin can have side effects, so don't use it unnecessarily or excessively. Most of the time, simple moist heat will relieve arthritic pain and soreness.

If you suffer from acute attacks of arthritis, ask your doctor about using aspirin. You know from reading Chapter 3 that it's usually not necessary to take more than two aspirin at a time for pain-relieving purposes. Let your doctor recommend an aspirin dosage for reducing inflammation in swollen joints.

THE ROLE OF DIET

There are many theories about the role of diet in arthritis, but as yet there is no concrete evidence that any one food will cause or cure arthritis. It is important, however, that you eat a good, balanced diet. And whenever possible, select fresh, natural foods rather than refined, artificial or chemically preserved foods.

The Dangers of Sugars and Starches

Some medical writers maintain that refined sugars and starches leave a toxic waste in the body that may cause arthritis by upsetting the body's calcium-phosphorus balance. In any event, it seems very likely that the cumulative effects of the chemicals in our foods may play a role in the development of some forms of arthritis.

The Healing Power of Ripe Cherries

There is some evidence to indicate that ripe cherries—or fresh cherry juice —may have a beneficial effect upon gout and arthritis. Whole cherries are also rich in pectin, which is believed to aid in the prevention of hardened arteries (See Chapter 5).

IMPROVING YOUR GENERAL HEALTH

Anything you can do to improve your general health will be helpful in combating arthritis. In addition to a good diet, you should get plenty of rest, fresh air, and sunshine, along with a moderate amount of exercise. It's especially important to avoid emotional stress and strain.

Turn back to Chapter 2 and study the measures recommended for overcoming nervous tension. Chapter 4, on how to relieve constipation, also contains some important health rules. Excessive use of mineral oil as a laxative, for example, can deprive your body of bone-building Vitamin D. Chapter 12 will tell you how to get maximum nourishment from your foods. You'll learn in that chapter that a deficiency in calcium can lead to a deficiency in Vitamin D and phosphorus, and vice versa. It's extremely important that your body not be deficient in any one of the vitamins and minerals known to be essential to health.

Try to establish regular working and sleeping hours so that your body will be able to function more efficiently. Persons who do "shift work," or who have no regular hours for eating, sleeping, working, playing, visiting the toilet, and so on, sometimes develop symptoms of stress that contribute to the development of the worst kind of arthritis.

Some forms of arthritis, such as those caused by emotional stress or a bad diet, will disappear whenever the mind and the body are restored to a healthy and balanced state. So don't take it for granted that your arthritis can't be cured. All you may have to do is to make a change in your way of life.

SUMMARY

1. Although some forms of arthritis cannot be cured, symptoms can be relieved and the disease controlled by observing certain self-help techniques.

2. Try to move arthritic joints through a full range of movement several times a day in order to prevent joint stiffness.

3. Make a special effort to sit, stand, and sleep with your joints straight and aligned in order to prevent joint irritation and muscle shortening.

4. You can relieve soreness and stiffness in an arthritic joint by applying moist heat in the form of hot compresses.

5. It may not be a good idea to massage directly over an acutely inflamed arthritic joint. Don't use vibrators or mechanical massagers.

6. If you have spinal arthritis, do straight-arm pullovers from an ottoman in order to straighten your spine and lift up your rib cage.

7. Simple aspirin is one of the safest and most effective medications for relieving the pain and inflammation of arthritis.

8. Eat a good, balanced diet, with emphasis on fresh, natural foods. Try to avoid refined, artificial, or chemically preserved foods.

9. Make a special effort to improve your general health by observing rules outlined in other chapters of this book.

8

Strike Out the Common Cold

Statistics tell us that the average person has about three colds each year. In the United States, the common cold takes the worker off the job more than any other illness. *Billions of dollars a year go down the drain in lost profits and wages*, and many millions of dollars are spent on *worthless* cold remedies.

Although the "common cold" is usually a self-limiting condition that rarely lasts longer than seven to ten days, it is obviously a serious problem. And because of its impact on the nation's economy, it deserves as much—or more —attention than some of our more "serious" illnesses.

Unfortunately, medical science has not yet found a cure for a cold infection. Attempts to use drugs and other forms of medication to shorten the course of a cold have proven to be futile and often harmful, since they sometimes prolong the disease by suppressing the symptoms. Drugs that constrict the mucous membranes to stop a runny nose, for example, may only interfere with the body's attempt to wash the infecting germs out of the body.

You can help yourself better by employing natural healing methods that help your body fight off the cold virus. If you follow all of the self-help techniques outlined in this chapter, you probably won't even develop a cold; but if you do, you can use the same techniques to relieve your symptoms and speed your recovery.

BODY RESISTANCE VERSUS COLD GERMS

Cold germs cannot normally invade the body until its resistance is weakened by certain disturbing influences. Once the germs do begin to multiply in the body, however, they become so strong and so bold that they are easily transmitted from one person to another, even to persons whose resistance is "normal." For this reason, you should stay away from persons who have colds.

If you develop a cold yourself, keep a safe distance from your friends and your family until your sneezing stops and the discharge from your nose is no longer thin and watery.

AVOIDING SECONDARY INFECTION

Once a cold begins, it must run its course. Prolonged infection in a run-down body, however, may allow secondary infection by more dangerous germs. This could result in pneumonia, strep throat, bronchitis, and other serious bacterial infections. So, it's important to take whatever steps may be necessary to speed your recovery from a cold.

HOW A DOCTOR PURGED HIMSELF OF COLDS

A doctor friend of mine who had been unsuccessful in curing his own colds with medication confessed that he didn't believe that anything could be done to prevent his annual winter cold. Each time he contracted the cold, it usually lasted so long that both of his nostrils were surrounded by scabs from constantly blowing his nose. After he spent several months observing the simple recommendations outlined in this chapter, however, he did not even have a cold the next winter!

"I should have known that my resistance was low," he said. "None of the medication I took ever did any good. And I just didn't know that you could control the cold germ by controlling the environment."

Pills won't do the job. You have to learn to help yourself.

DON'T WAIT FOR A "COLD CURE"

Don't wait around for the development of a "miracle drug" that will cure or prevent a cold. Since there are hundreds of different cold viruses that may break through weak body defenses to cause a cold, there may never be a completely effective drug treatment for colds.

BUILDING RESISTANCE AGAINST COLDS

If you observe the health-building suggestions outlined in other chapters of this book, you'll go a long way toward preventing colds. Nervous tension, constipation, and other disturbing influences, for example, are all part of a complex chain of events that leads to lowered resistance. But if you want to build maximum resistance against the cold germ, you must not fail to observe the rules outlined in this chapter.

The Importance of Diet

You'll learn in Chapter 12 that a deficiency of either Vitamin A or Vitamin C—or both—can lead to increased susceptibility to all kinds of infections, including colds.

DOUBLING UP ON VITAMIN C: If you have frequent colds in spite of eating a balanced diet, you should make a special effort to increase your intake of foods that are rich in Vitamin C. Try to drink a glass of orange juice or tomato juice each morning. Whenever possible, flavor tea, fish, and other appropriate foods with fresh lemon juice. Drink lemonade instead of tea with your evening meal. Include an orange, a tangerine, or a piece of grapefruit in your between-meal snacks. There are, of course, other sources of Vitamin C, but acid fruits—citrus fruits in particular—are usually best.

Remember that your body doesn't store Vitamin C beyond its immediate needs. This means that you must eat something every day that's rich in this important vitamin.

Getting Adequate Rest

Your body's ability to resist the cold virus depends to a large extent upon the rest you get. This doesn't mean that the more rest you get the stronger your resistance will be. It does mean, however, that you should get all the rest you need, particularly sleep.

Whenever fatigue overtakes you, slow down and rest until your energy level is restored. If your body doesn't get enough rest and sleep to recuperate from the stress and strains of each day, your resistance may become so low that disease germs will be able to march right into the cells of your body like an invading army.

Moderation in Exercise

Regular exercise is essential in building resistance against infection, since it stimulates the circulation of blood as well as the various body functions. But don't overdo it. Too much exercise can produce fatigue that will temporarily lower body resistance.

Whatever type of exercise you do, begin lightly and progressively. Don't push yourself to the point of exhaustion. Chapter 13 will tell you how you can stimulate the circulation of blood without taking exercise.

Keeping a Tranquil Mind

Whenever you find yourself depressed and in a rut, make whatever changes may be necessary to restore a better mental attitude. The more unhappy you are, the more likely it is that you'll catch a cold. It seems that a case of "blues" can disturb the mucous membranes in such away that they're less resistant to infection. Lab studies have already revealed that emotional upsets can result in a chemical change in the nose to create a more favorable environment for the growth of virus and bacteria.

Bright lights might also have some effect on the membranes of the nose. Did you ever sneeze after looking up at the sun? This is a nerve reflex that momentarily tickles the lining of the nose. A similar reflex may be generated by a disturbing state of mind.

THE CASE OF THE UNHAPPY DIVORCEE: I knew an intelligent young divorcee who suffered from chronic colds in spite of her efforts to live a healthy life. When she remarried and was assured of security for herself and her children, her colds disappeared.

Breathe Clean Air

Stale air in closed, poorly ventilated rooms contains germs that are breathed in and out of the lungs many times. Germs cling to dust particles and literally ride from the floor into your lungs. Cold germs are easily spread during the winter when large numbers of people in offices and factories close windows and doors and breathe the same air.

Oxygen kills germs. The better the ventilation, the more oxygen in the air. Try to breathe fresh air so that each breath you take will clean your lungs.

Chapter 14 will tell you more about breathing for better health.

AVOIDING IRRITATIONS THAT BREAK DOWN YOUR COLD DEFENSE

Medical records indicate that most colds occur in autumn, midwinter, and spring, with a peak in midwinter. The viruses that cause cold symptoms are, of course, present during the entire year. But they are more of a threat during seasons in which the body is subjected to sudden and extreme changes in temperature.

Medical scientists have known for a long time that chilling the body causes reflex constriction of the tiny blood vessels supplying the mucous membranes of the nose and throat. When the cold viruses were finally discovered with the aid of an electron microscope, it was found that these tiny and elusive little germs could invade the constricted membranes under certain conditions.

Resistance Is Lowered by Chills

Whenever the seasons begin to change, it's difficult to avoid an occasional chill. In the spring, for example, when the days and nights are not consistently warm or cold, you may be caught without adequate clothing or cover. In the winter, most of us live and work in hot, stuffy shops and offices and then dash out into the cold to shock sensitive membranes in the nose and throat.

Chilling also occurs in the summer when air conditioning is allowed to blow over the feet or when swimmers become fatigued in cold water.

One of the surest ways to catch cold is to step from a warm shower into a draft of cold air. Taking out the garbage or bringing in the laundry while only partially dressed is a common cause of cold in spring and fall.

How to Avoid Getting Chilled

Try to anticipate temperature changes so that you can prepare for them. Don't overheat your home in the winter. When you go outdoors in cold weather dress warmly so your body won't be shocked by a sudden change in temperature. Don't overdress, however, to the extent that your body perspires from overheating. When you come back indoors, remove the heavy clothing so that you'll remain comfortable.

If the weather is extremely cold, you can reduce the shock of breathing icy air by holding a handkerchief over your nose until the membranes of your nose and throat have time to adjust to the temperature change.

If you think it might turn cool during the night, keep an extra blanket close by so that you can reach out for it if you need it. Don't lie in bed chilled and half asleep waiting for the alarm to go off.

Always keep your feet covered when you're in an air-conditioned room. When your feet are chilled, the membranes in your throat are so badly constricted that your throat may be dry and raspy only moments after the exposure.

COLD AIR ON A WET BODY: During the summer, some people catch cold by walking into an air-conditioned room while perspiring. Remember that a perspiring skin can be chilled quite easily by currents of cool air. All of us have had the experience of developing nasal congestion after sitting under a fan. If body resistance is not low enough to permit invasion by cold germs, the congestion usually disappears after a few hours.

"COLDS" CAUSED BY ALLERGY: Most "summer colds" are caused by allergies. If you develop a cold that seems to last through the summer, see your doctor.

GRADUATING YOUR SHOWER: Whenever you take a shower, always finish up by gradually turning down the warm water as you turn up the cold water. You don't have to torture yourself with an extremely cold shower, however. In fact, a too-cold shower will only lower your resistance by shocking your body. Just reduce the temperature of the water until it's comfortably cool. This will close the pores of your skin as well as protect your body from cooling drafts when you get out of the shower.

Taking extremely cold showers will not increase your resistance against colds. It may be possible, however, to increase your tolerance to fairly cold water by gradually exposing your body to colder water. This might provide some protection for athletes and other persons who must enter the water on cold days.

If you have high blood pressure, you should probably avoid very cold showers, since cold water may further raise your blood pressure by constricting your blood vessels.

GETTING ACCUSTOMED TO COLD WEATHER: The story is told of the well-clothed plainsman who asked a scantily-clad Indian why he didn't cover all of his body in cool weather. The Indian, in turn, asked the plainsman why he didn't cover his face. "My face is used to it," the plainsman answered. "Ugh. Me all face," the Indian replied.

Since most of us live and work with almost complete protection against the elements, with little or no exposure to gradual changes in weather, it has become necessary to protect our bodies against even minor changes in temperature. None of us can afford to be a weekend Indian.

Avoiding Exposure to Cold Germs

If cold germs are not in your body or in the air you breathe, you won't develop a cold, no matter how low your resistance may get. Unless you live in arctic regions, however, where cold germs are not normally present in the atmosphere, you'll be forever exposed to these germs. And the minute you drop your guard, in come the germs.

KEEPING YOUR DISTANCE: Even if you stay healthy and keep your resistance up, you'll have to stay away from persons who have colds if you don't want to "catch" their cold. Sneezing and coughing spreads germs several feet in all directions. So keep your distance.

DON'T KISS THE BRIDE! That is, unless you're the bridegroom—and only then if you don't have a cold. More than one lovely and eager bride has had her honeymoon ruined by a cold transmitted to her from the kiss of a well-wisher.

AVOIDING CONTAMINATED OBJECTS: Don't ever use a napkin, glass, plate, fork, or any other personal object that has been used (and not washed) by a person with a cold. Cold germs are also able to survive in unwashed blankets, towels, and other dry articles that have been used or handled by infected persons.

A group of arctic explorers who failed to develop the symptoms of a cold in spite of fatigue, hardship, and chilling did develop the disease after using blankets shipped to them from the United States. They then transmitted the infection to Eskimos who had never had a cold.

DON'T BLOW OUT THE CANDLES ON A BIRTHDAY CAKE! How many times have you eaten a piece of cake after someone huffed and puffed to blow out the candles on the top layer? Did you ever stop to think that you were also ingesting the other person's germs? Don't ever let anyone blow out the candles on *your* birthday cake.

RELIEVING SYMPTOMS AND FIGHTING OFF A COLD

If you contract a cold in spite of everything you do to prevent it, there are several things you can do to relieve your discomfort and help your body overcome the infection.

Stay Home and Rest

When a cold first begins, your nose and throat may feel dry, swollen, and raspy. Heed this cue to stay home and rest in a room where the temperature is comfortable.

Take a Hot Bath and Get into a Warm Bed

Soaking in a tub of hot water, followed by rest in a warm bed, will increase the circulation of blood and stimulate your body defenses. If there's any chance of being exposed to drafts of cool air when you leave the bathroom, however, you should finish with a comfortably cool shower.

Drink Hot Liquids

Hot drinks will stimulate the circulation of blood through the mucous membranes of the nose and throat.

IRISH MOSS LEMONADE will provide soothing relief for colds and sore throats. Wash a quarter cup of Irish moss (a dried seaweed that's also called "carrageen") and let it soak for 15 minutes. Then drain the water, add two cups of cold water, and cook in the top of a double boiler for about 20 minutes, or until it becomes syrupy. If it becomes too thick, add hot water. Strain the liquid and add four tablespoons of lemon juice and enough sugar to suit your taste. Reheat if necessary.

Irish moss is found mostly on the rocky Atlantic coast, but it may also be purchased in some health food stores. Some persons grow their own moss in backyard rock gardens.

Eat Lightly—But Eat!

Eat what you feel you want to eat, but don't overeat. If the stomach is forced to digest a big meal, much of the body's blood supply must be concentrated upon digestion rather than upon fighting the cold virus.

Go easy on concentrated sweets and fats. You know from reading other chapters in this book that refined sweets will ultimately lower your blood sugar and decrease your energy by overstimulating your pancreas and depriving your body of Vitamin B. Fat and greasy foods are so difficult to digest that they may place a strain on both your body metabolism and your digestion.

Try to eat fresh, natural, easy-to-digest foods—especially fruits.

Drink Plenty of Liquids

Most doctors will tell you to drink several glasses of water each day in order to replace the fluids lost to fever and the stepped-up secretion of mucous. You should avoid cold drinks, however, since they will shock already inflamed throat tissues.

Saturate Your Body with Vitamin C

If your body is not actually deficient in Vitamin C, no one can guarantee you that an increased intake of this vitamin will cure your cold. But there is some evidence to indicate that saturating your blood with Vitamin C tends to shut out the cold virus just as effectively as penicillin can arrest the multiplication of bacteria. The body may then make some headway in overcoming the already entrenched virus while preventing invasion by new virus.

Since the juice of citrus fruits is rich in Vitamin C, you can get both your vitamins and your liquids from fruit juice. The juice of a freshly squeezed orange is much more palatable than a vitamin pill and a glass of water.

Don't worry about your blood becoming "acid" from drinking large quantities of fruit juice. All acid fruits have an *alkaline* reaction in the body, and they help cleanse the system by stimulating the function of both the bowels and the kidneys.

A Little "Nip" Might Help

Believe it or not, there are some authorities who maintain that a heated alcoholic drink may prevent the development of a bad cold infection. They maintain that a small amount of alcohol will dilate blood vessels that have been constricted by a chill, thus normalizing the circulation. If this is the case, a "hot toddy" may prove to be an effective medication in the early stages of a cold.

In addition to its effect upon blood circulation, the alcohol may actually kill the germs it comes into contact with in the throat.

Remember, though, that alcohol is a potentially dangerous drug if used excessively.

Go Easy on Coffee and Cigarettes

Unlike alcohol, which is a vasodilator (expands the veins), the caffeine in coffee constricts the veins. A cup of coffee might initially increase the circulation of blood through the membranes of the throat by heating them directly. But once the caffeine is absorbed into the system, it might do more harm than good by constricting the blood vessels.

Just recently, doctors discovered that a woman who had had a chronic cold for years was drinking dozens of cups of coffee each day. When she quit drinking coffee, her cold disappeared. Apparently, the drug-like effect of the caffeine had restricted the circulation of blood to such an extent that she was constantly vulnerable to infection by cold virus.

Strangely enough, some cold remedies contain caffeine in spite of the fact that it appears to weaken body resistance.

Cigarettes are also vasoconstrictors. The nicotine in the smoke of a single cigarette can constrict tiny blood vessels all over your body. The smoke itself is irritating to the membranes of the nose, throat, and lungs.

Humidify Your Room

Medical scientists tell us that increased moisture in the air weakens the cold virus, while hot, dry air contributes to the development of a cold.

Ordinarily, your nose warms and moistens the air you breathe in order to prevent drying of your lungs. But if the air is too dry from the use of room heaters, your nose will become dry and irritated and the cilia (tiny hair-like bits of living tissue that are constantly whipping back and forth to push mucous, germs, dust, and other debris out of the lungs) that line the tubes leading to your lungs won't function efficiently. The mucous membranes in your nose and throat may also "crack" to let the cold germs through. For this reason, it might be a good idea to humidify your bedroom during the winter. You can do this with a commercial vaporizer that heats a little salty water.

MEASURING RELATIVE HUMIDITY: Experiments indicate that a relative humidity of about 45 percent is best for most persons. You can calculate humidity by comparing readings from a wet-bulb and a dry-bulb thermometer. The closer together the readings are, the higher the humidity.

You can purchase a unit called a "psychrometer" that contains both wet-bulb and dry-bulb thermometers for a precalculated daily reading of the amount of moisture in the air.

Steam Inhalation

Breathing steam from a pot of boiling water will open clogged nostrils, loosen thick mucous, stimulate circulation, and free the cilia so that germ-laden mucous can be expelled by blowing your nose.

Breathe the steam for a few minutes at a time, several times a day. Simply breathing concentrated moisture may, in some cases, halt an early cold infection by arresting the multiplication of cold virus.

You can humidify your bathroom for a quick "steam room" by turning on a hot shower full blast.

KILLING COLD GERMS WITH ACID VAPORS: Did you know that during a cold infection the mucous of the nose changes from acid to alkaline? The nose is normally acid, and we know that an acid environment is unfavorable to the growth of cold germs.

If ways can be found to keep the secretions of the nose slightly acid, many colds could probably be prevented. Steam inhalation and nose sprays with a slightly acid content might be helpful. The acid in fruit juices may help kill germs in the throat. This may be one reason why citrus fruits seem to be beneficial in the treatment and prevention of colds.

Try heating a water and vinegar mixture until it begins to steam and then inhale the vapors. Put in just enough vinegar to give off mildly acid fumes.

Stopping Colds with Garlic

Eating garlic or drinking water containing garlic oil has been shown to be effective in preventing the development of a cold. Water and garlic oil may also be vaporized and inhaled. The strong aromatic effect of garlic acts as a natural germicide.

Try a Moist Chest Pack

Hot packs or a mustard plaster on the chest will help relieve congestion and speed recovery from a chest cold. See Chapter 7 for instructions on how to make hot compresses and a mustard plaster.

KEEP YOUR TONSILS!

Not too many years ago, doctors routinely removed the tonsils and adenoids of children, "since they would eventually have to come out anyway"— or so they thought. Today, we know that the tonsils are part of a protective ring of lymphatic tissue that surrounds and guards the nose and throat against invasion by disease germs. Whenever the tonsils become sore from filtering out and destroying these germs, this doesn't mean that they must be removed. It just means they're doing their job.

Nowadays, few doctors will take out the tonsils unless they are badly infected or extremely enlarged. If you can manage to keep your tonsils, you'll have a better defense against cold infection.

HOW TO BLOW YOUR NOSE

The mucous membranes of a healthy upper respiratory tract secrete about a quart of fluid each day. Most of this is evaporated into the air drawn into the lungs in a marvelous air-conditioning effect. Some of it is expelled along with dust and other particles that are captured and pushed out by the cilia. Whenever the membranes are irritated or infected, however, copious amounts of fluid may be secreted in the body's effort to "clean" the membranes or wash out the infection. This results in the all-too-familiar runny nose.

When a cold passes through the watery and mucous stages, the fluids become thick and sticky. This requires a considerable amount of nose-blowing to keep the air passages open. And if it isn't done properly, it can lead to trouble.

Don't blow your nose too hard. Leave both nostrils open. Closing one side of your nose may cause a back-up of pressure that will force cold germs back through a small passageway that connects the inner ear with the portion of the throat just behind the nose. If this happens, a painful and serious ear infection may result.

If your nose ever stops up completely, breathe a little steam vapor to loosen the mucous. *Don't ever close both nostrils together in order to build up pressure for explosive expulsion of stubborn or dried mucous.*

DON'T PUT COLD GERMS INTO YOUR POCKET: Every time you blow your nose during the watery stage of a cold, you fill your handkerchief with cold germs. Try to use paper napkins or tissues so that you can discard the germs when you discard the napkin or tissues.

Even when a handkerchief is dry, it can spread cold germs when it's pulled from the pocket and shaken in the air; that is, of course, if it has been used by someone suffering from a cold.

IF YOU DEVELOP A FEVER AND OTHER COMPLICATIONS...

If you take care of yourself when a cold begins, chances are you'll make a full recovery in less than a week with no complications. However, if you develop a fever, a pain in your head or chest, or other symptoms indicating bacterial infection, or if your cold lasts longer than two weeks, see your doctor.

Sinusitis, bronchitis, strep throat, tonsillitis, influenza, pneumonia, and other diseases caused by bacteria that have invaded a body weakened by the common cold can be serious or even fatal. It may be necessary for your doctor to prescribe a specific drug that will paralyze or destroy the bacteria until the body can recover and rebuild its defenses.

THE DANGERS OF COLD REMEDIES

You already know that there is no medication that will cure a cold. In fact, some of the popular drug-type "cold cures" can make a cold worse or result in harmful side effects. At their best, patent medicines provide only temporary relief from the symptoms of a cold.

The Effect of Antihistamine

Medical scientists tell us that antihistamine has no beneficial effect in curing or relieving a cold, and that it is used primarily in the treatment of allergies. Yet, this drug is found in almost all of the over-the-counter cold remedies.

Antihistamine makes some persons sleepy or dizzy. It can even impair judgment or cause headache, possibly causing auto accidents or plane crashes.

What Aspirin Can Do for a Cold

Aspirin is a common ingredient of cold remedies. This useful drug will relieve your aches and pains to some extent, thus making you feel better. It may also reduce your fever. But even aspirin can have side effects, and it provides only temporary relief from symptoms.

If your cold makes you so miserable that you feel you need some relief from symptoms, aspirin by itself is the only known medication that can do the job with a reasonable amount of safety. If it causes nausea, vomiting, diarrhea, dizziness, or any other disturbance, however, its use should be discontinued.

If you have a stomach ulcer or any kind of inflammation in your stomach or intestinal tract, the acid in an aspirin can worsen your condition by eroding the raw surfaces.

Decongestants

There is another more powerful drug in some cold remedies that can temporarily open a stuffy nose by constricting tiny blood vessels and shrinking the swollen membranes inside the nose. It acts very much like adrenalin. But when the effect of the drug wears off, the congestion returns and it may be worse than before.

Stopping the flow of mucous from the nose during the acute stages of a cold infection may simply retard the cleansing process and prolong the cold.

Should You Take Antibiotics?

Cold tablets, cough drops, and throat lozenges that contain traces of sulfa drugs or antibiotics can be dangerous. The drug-content of such medication is usually too small to kill germs but enough to result in an allergic reaction in the mouth and throat. They should be used only in treating severe bacterial infections.

Don't ask your doctor for penicillin when you have a cold. This drug has no effect at all upon cold virus.

SUMMARY

1. Build and maintain good health by eating a balanced diet, getting adequate rest, taking regular exercise, and maintaining a tranquil mind.

2. Increase your intake of foods rich in Vitamin A and Vitamin C. Fish liver oil is a good source of Vitamin A. Citrus fruit or strawberries offer a rich source of Vitamin C.

3. Always dress in such a way that your body won't be shocked by sudden changes in temperature.

4. Don't overheat your home in the winter. Try to adjust room temperature to about 72 degrees Fahrenheit with a relative humidity of about 45 percent.

5. Always finish your shower by turning down the hot water and turning up the cold water until the water is comfortably cool.

6. Don't sit under the direct air currents of a fan. Always keep your feet covered in an air-conditioned room.

7. When a cold strikes, stay home, stay warm, drink hot liquids, eat fresh fruits and vegetables, and breathe a little steam vapor spiked with vinegar.

8. Leave both nostrils open when you blow your nose so you won't force cold germs into your inner ear.

9. Don't waste your money on "cold cures." Some of them may relieve your symptoms but prolong your cold.

Use Home Treatment to Cure Your Backache

Mrs. Susan D. suffered from chronic backache. Her back hurt when she went to bed at night and it hurt when she got up in the morning.

"My back has been bothering me for years," she said. "My doctor says that nothing can be done and that I'll just have to learn to live with it. But I've got to do something. I'm getting so nervous and grouchy that I'm a terror to live with."

Sound familiar?

Mr. Randy C. had never had a backache in his life. But one day while he was unloading an air conditioner from a pickup truck, he strained his back.

"I haven't been able to work for the past two weeks," he complained, "and I can't afford to lose that much pay. If I don't go back to work soon I'll be in trouble. Is there anything I can do to speed my recovery and make sure that I don't hurt my back again?"

I instructed both of these people in the simple self-help techniques described in this chapter. Both made a complete recovery, and neither had a recurrence of back trouble.

BACKACHE IS A COMMON AILMENT

One out of every three persons suffers from backache. Among those who must work for a living, however, *back trouble is second only to heart disease as the most common cause of work loss caused by chronic disability.* (See Figure 9-1.)

About 28 million people visit doctors each year in search of relief from backache. Medical records indicate that backache is even more common than headache and other "common" ailments. But don't despair. Like many other

Figure 9-1. Most backaches occur in the lumbar portion of the back and spine.

chronic disorders, backache can be relieved with simple self-help techniques. Regardless of the type of back trouble you may have, you can eliminate the need for expensive treatment or medication by following certain basic rules.

If your backache should persist or grow worse, you should, of course, seek the advice of a specialist, but you'll still have to know how to take care of your back in order to prevent chronic disability.

COMMON CAUSES OF BACKACHE AND BACK STRAIN

There are two major causes of backache and back strain: improper lifting techniques and poor posture. Other common causes may be nervous tension and lack of exercise.

You should, of course, strengthen your back muscles with exercise. But if you lift improperly or sit and stand incorrectly, you'll subject your joints and ligaments to damaging strain, no matter how strong your muscles may be.

HOW IMPROPER LIFTING CAN STRAIN YOUR BACK

Bill H. was a weightlifter who had developed very powerful muscles by exercising with barbells and dumbbells. He lifted heavy weights in his workouts, but he never hurt his back. One day while he was lifting a spare tire out of the trunk of his car, he strained his back.

"How could I strain myself lifting such a light weight?" he asked. "I've got a strong back."

I explained to Bill that when you lift with your back instead of with your legs, you're using your spine as a lever, and this puts your lower back in a vulnerable position.

How to Lift with Your Legs

Unfortunately, many people do not seem to know how to lift with their legs—or their legs are too weak to do so. If you can't do a full squat with your back straight up and down and your hands on your hips, you should strengthen your legs by doing squatting exercises.

Four Important Lifting Rules

Observe these rules every time you lift an object or pick something up from the floor.

1. Stand close to the object you want to lift. Place your feet in a comfortable, parallel stance.

2. Keep your feet flat on the floor and squat down with your back flat and as vertical as possible. (See Figure 9-2.)

Figure 9-2. Always keep your back flat and lift with your legs.

3. Lift the object by straightening your legs; that is, by standing erect while keeping your spine straight and erect.

4. Keep the object you're lifting close to your body in order to avoid placing leverage on your spine. Once the object has been lifted, let it rest against your body. (See Figure 9-3.)

How to Place a Heavy Object on a Table

If you want to place a heavy object on a high table, first place it on a waist-high table by using the lifting technique described above. Then squat down

Figure 9-3. When carrying a heavy object, always let it rest against your body.

with your back straight and clamp the object against your chest so that you can place it on the higher table when you stand erect.

WARNING: Always face the object you intend to lift so that you can lift it straight up. You could strain you back severely if you should turn, twist, or bend while lifting.

THE IMPORTANCE OF GOOD POSTURE

How you sit and stand during the day can have a great deal to do with how your back feels. If you slump at a desk or lean over a work bench, for example, your back will begin to ache within minutes. And if you maintain such tiring postures day in and day out, you'll develop spinal distortions, tight muscles and chronic irritations that will result in *constant* backache.

Correcting Backache with a Change in Posture

A 34-year-old insurance executive who complained of backache and leg ache after sitting at his desk all day was able to relieve his symptoms by getting rid of his overstuffed office chair and taking time out several times a day to practice good standing posture.

"I used to think that my backache was caused by kidney trouble," he confessed, "but those kidney pills never seemed to help. Those posture exercises certainly did the trick."

Like many Americans who suffer from backache, the insurance executive was the victim of stress and tension that was compounded by static and im-

If you must sit or stand most of the day in the type of work you do, it's imperative that you observe the rules of good posture. You should also make a special effort to move about frequently in order to relieve tension on taut and fatigued muscles.

Good, dynamic posture is important in both the treatment and prevention of backache. Try to develop the habit of sitting and standing correctly at all times.

Figure 9-4. A chair that is too high to let the feet rest flat on the floor will place damaging pressure on nerves and blood vessels behind the knee.

How to Sit Correctly

Bad sitting posture can do more than give you a backache—it can also cause hip and leg pain. Since most of us sit more than we stand each day, let's first consider the rules of good sitting posture.

SELECTING A CHAIR: The type of chair you use and the sitting posture you assume should depend largely upon whether you're relaxing or working. When you're working, you should use an upright straight-back chair. But when you're relaxing, the back of the chair may slant backward a little, and it should be molded to the normal curves of your spine.

You can place a folded towel in the small of your back for a little extra support when you drive a car.

Whenever you're sitting in an armless straight-back chair, you should sit far enough back in the chair to touch your buttocks against the chair-back. Then sit erect so that there is a hollow in your lower back.

CHAIR HEIGHT IS IMPORTANT: Select a chair that's just high enough to let both of your feet rest flat on the floor with only a slight amount of pressure against the back of your thighs. If the chair is too high, your feet will dangle and the front edge of the chair will cut into the back of your thighs. This can obstruct the flow of blood to your legs and place a damaging pressure on the big sciatic nerve to cause numbness and leg pain. (See Figure 9-4.)

If the chair is too low, the knees will be thrust upward and the normal curve of the lower spine will be reversed. This can be fatiguing for the hips as well as the back.

If you slump excessively and sit on the end of your spine rather than on your buttocks, you may develop a painful tailbone.

How to Stand Properly

Not everyone can stand exactly the same way, but there are certain basic rules that everyone can follow in building good posture. (See Figure 9-5.)

Figure 9-5. Improper standing posture can develop a permanent and ugly hump in the back.

Stand in front of a mirror and practice the posture drill that follows until you can assume good, erect posture without even thinking about it.

Five Postural Exercises

1. Stand tall, as if you were trying to increase your height a little.

2. Lift your chest up, pull your shoulders back, and pull your abdomen in just a little. You should be able to keep your abdomen flat and your shoulders square with very little effort and still be able to breathe and move about normally. Let your arms hang loosely at your sides.

3. Point your toes nearly straight ahead. It's all right for your feet to point slightly outward, but you should try to avoid standing slew-footed or pigeon-toed.

4. Lift your arches up a little so that your weight is supported on the out-side edges of the soles of your feet. This will keep your ankles from rolling inward (Chapter 10).

5. Observe your posture from the side. If there is a deep hollow in your lower back and your buttocks are prominent, tuck your hips under a little to balance the normal curves of your spine.

OVERWORK A COMMON CAUSE OF BACKACHE

If you work hard for a living, you may suffer from job-related backache in spite of all you do to prevent it. There's a great deal that you can do at

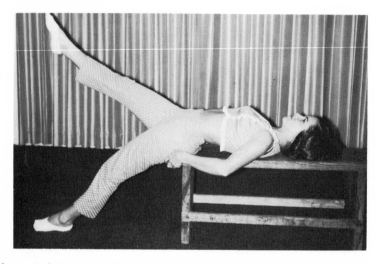

Figure 9-6. Persons who sit a lot should do this scissors exercise to stretch hip flexors and hamstrings.

home to relieve your symptoms, but the type of treatment you use should depend upon the type of work you do. If you sit or stand all day in an office or a factory, for example, you may be able to relieve your backache by taking a little exercise. But if you perform labor during the day, you may get more relief by resting and using heat and massage.

Classify the type of work you do and then try the self-help measures recommended for the type of backache associated with such work.

If your backache becomes worse, or if any part of the treatment proves to be painful, see your doctor.

RELIEVING BACKACHE CAUSED BY PROLONGED SITTING OR STANDING

Sitting and standing for long hours at a time is probably the most common cause of after-work backache. Postural strains which restrict movement are more likely to cause backache than work that permits a great deal of movement.

Almost any kind of exercise that moves the joints freely, such as swimming, handball, calisthenics, and so on, will relieve backache caused by inactivity and static posture. An "exercise break" during working hours may even prevent backache. Try to take a little exercise immediately after work in order to relieve your aches, pains, and tensions before you sit down for your evening meal.

How Sitting Affects Your Muscles

In any sitting posture, the muscles on the front of the hips and on the back of the thighs shorten to accommodate the bend in the hips and the knees. If such posture is maintained day after day, these muscles may become permanently short. Then, when you stand erect, the tension in the muscles pulls on your back and legs.

The Case of the Stool Sitter

A machine operator in a paper mill complained of backache and leg ache that seemed to be aggravated by standing erect. A thorough medical examination had already ruled out organic disease. When I questioned him about his work, he told me that he sat on a high stool so that he could brace his forearms on his thighs. Many years of sitting in this posture had resulted in shortening of both his hamstrings and his hip flexors. This made it difficult for him to assume a normal, relaxed standing posture.

Two Special Exercises for Stretching Tight Hip and Thigh Muscles

Do these exercises to relieve stiffness caused by too much sitting. They worked for the machine operator and they'll work for you.

1. **LEG SCISSORS FROM A BENCH:** Lie on your back on a low bench with your legs locked out straight and your heels resting on the floor. Keep both legs straight and raise one leg as high as you can while keeping the heel of the opposite foot on the floor. Exercise both legs equally for several repetitions. (See Figure 9-6.)

2. **THE GOOD-MORNING EXERCISE:** Stand erect with your legs straight and your hands on your hips. *Keep your back flat and your head up* and bend forward until you feel a pull on the back of your legs. (See Figure 9-7.)

Figure 9-7. Bending forward with the legs straight will stretch hamstrings without placing pressure on the lumbar discs.

Do this exercise slowly and cautiously. Fast or forceful movement could result in "pulled" hamstrings or a sacroiliac strain. Don't do this exercise at all if you have back trouble or if it causes back or leg pain. Several repetitions should be adequate.

BEWARE OF TOE-TOUCHING EXERCISES!

If you do toe-touching exercises, be careful not to do them so rapidly that momentum causes you to "bounce" at the bottom of the exercise. The muscles on the back of your legs may pull against your pelvis and cause a back strain when the spine moves into a flexed position. A great deal of pressure would also be placed on the discs at the bottom of the spine.

Toe-touching with straight legs will increase your flexibility by stretching your hamstrings, but more harm than good can result if the exercise isn't performed properly. It really isn't necessary to touch your toes, so don't try to do so forcefully. Do the exercise slowly, letting the weight of the upper body do the stretching.

RELIEVING BACKACHE CAUSED BY OVEREXERTION

If you spend the day loading trucks, digging ditches, shoveling snow, working in a construction crew, landscaping your lawn, or doing any kind of work in which heavy muscular exertion is required, you may end up with a backache; and if you're not accustomed to such work, your backache may be acute.

Since your back muscles have already been overworked by the day's labor, you need rest rather than exercise, so you'll probably want to relax when you get home. But you can rest a lot better if you first use a few simple home-treatment techniques to relieve your aches and pains.

A Special Home-Treatment Routine for Overworked Backs

1. Have someone apply *moist heat* to your back for about 15 minutes. (See Figure 9-8.)

You can make a good hot compress by filling a hot water bottle with hot faucet water and then wrapping it in a piece of flannel that has been wrung out in hot water. Place the compress over the aching portion of your back and then cover both your back and the compress with a sheet of plastic to hold in the heat.

2. Follow the application of heat with *stroking massage.*

Your partner should start at the bottom of your spine near your hips. He places one hand on each side of your spine, with his thumbs in the center of your back and his fingers slanted off on each side so that his hands are molded to the ridges of muscle that run up and down your back. Then, with a firm pressure, he strokes slowly and smoothly toward your head, moving both hands together about five or six inches up your back. Each stroke should be finished by sliding the hands off to the side so that the thumbs move over

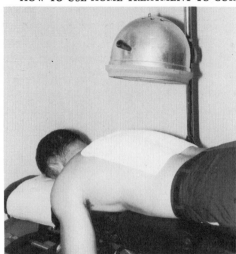

Figure 9-8. Moist heat applied with a damp towel and an infrared lamp is an effective backache treatment.

and across the ridges of muscle. The strokes should be overlapped until the entire length of the back has been massaged. The massage may be repeated two or three times if desired. (See Figure 9-9.)

Figure 9-9. The ridges of muscle on either side of the spine should be massaged from bottom to top.

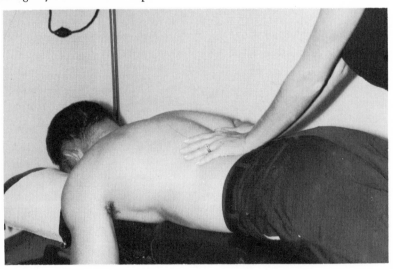

A small amount of oil should be used on the skin to reduce friction and to prevent irritation. When the massage has been completed, the oil may be removed with rubbing alcohol. If you have dry skin, just wipe the back with a dry cloth so that some of the oil will remain on the skin.

3. Stand up and bend your trunk from side to side several times. The *light muscular contraction* will aid the heat and massage in pumping out the irritating waste products that have accumulated in your overworked back muscles.

4. Get down on your hands and knees and lift your back up and down in order to *loosen your vertebrae*; that is, lift your back up to form a hump and then drop it down as far as it will go. (See Figures 9-10 and 9-11.)

5. Take a *hot shower* and then gradually reduce the temperature of the water until it's *comfortably cool*. Let the water play over the aching portion of your back in a thick, heavy stream.

6. After your body has been dried with a towel, have someone apply a *skin-warming liniment* (such as oil of wintergreen) to your back before you get dressed.

ICE MASSAGE FOR INFLAMED MUSCLES

If you develop a muscular backache that isn't relieved by heat, try using ice massage or a cold pack. Cold has been found to be effective in relieving certain types of muscular inflammation.

How to Massage with Ice

Freeze a paper cup full of water. Then peel the paper from the ice so that you'll have an icy cylinder. Put a small amount of oil on the skin in order to lessen the shock of the cold and then rub the ice up and down the affected muscles with a firm pressure. The massage should be applied for five or six minutes or until the skin is numbed by the cold.

If the pain returns after the effects of the cold wear off, repeat the massage.

You can protect your hands from the cold by wearing gloves—or you may freeze an ice cream stick in one end of the ice so that you can hold onto the stick rather than the ice.

Figures 9-10 and 9-11. To stretch muscles and loosen vertebrae, drop your back down as far as you can and then arch it up into a hump.

How to Make a Cold Compress

Fill a rubber bottle or a plastic container with crushed ice and then wrap it in a moist towel before applying it to the back. Cover all this with a sheet of plastic to prevent the circulation of air. Leave the application on for 20 to 30 minutes or until the pain eases.

AVOID OVERWORK WHENEVER POSSIBLE

Always try to avoid working too long in heavy work that you aren't accustomed to performing. If you take a new job calling for a great deal of muscular effort, start out by working only half a day for the first few days, especially if you aren't in good physical condition. Gradually increase the amount of work you do from day to day.

If you should suffer a back injury that takes you off the job for several days, you'll have to begin working lightly and progressively in order to prevent recurrence of the injury. Your back muscles must regain their strength before they're forced to assume a full work load.

SLEEP ON A FIRM MATTRESS

Everyone should sleep on a firm mattress. If you have back trouble, it's even more important that you have a good mattress. You should not expect to get rid of your back pain if you retire each night to a sagging mattress. Lack of firm support for your spine while your muscles are relaxed in the various sleeping postures will place a great deal of strain on the spinal joints and their ligaments. This by itself can cause backache; and if your back is already sore and inflamed from stress and strain, your trouble may be made worse rather than better with "bed rest."

If your back is hurting when you get up in the morning and you don't have spinal arthritis, there's a good possibility that your mattress sags too much.

A simple cotton, felt, or hair-stuffed mattress, if evenly packed, will be best for most persons. An inner-spring mattress may be all right if the springs can mold themselves to the contours of the body and still keep the spine aligned horizontally.

If the mattress you now have seems to sag too much, you can firm it up with a bed board.

Blueprint for a Bed Board

A one-half-inch-thick sheet of plywood that has been cut to the same length and width as your bed springs will keep your mattress from sagging. Just insert the board *between* the mattress and the springs.

Some people misunderstand their doctor when he says "sleep on a board," and mistakenly put the board on top of the mattress instead of under it.

Don't Make Your Mattress too Hard!

It is, of course, possible to make a mattress too hard. No mattress should be so firm that it cannot mold itself to the normal curves of the spine. Persons who try to sleep on a floor mat whenever they have a backache may aggravate their trouble by forcing their spine to straighten out too much.

USING A PILLOW TO EASE BACKACHE TENSION

As a rule, the best way to sleep is flat on your back. But if you have an acute backache, you may find that lying with your legs flat on the mattress will increase your discomfort. Whenever this is the case, put a pillow under your knees so that you can lie relaxed with your knees bent. This will relieve the pull of your hip-flexor muscles on your lower spine. It will also relieve tension in your hamstrings (on the back of your legs) so that you can lie perfectly relaxed. (See Figure 9-12.)

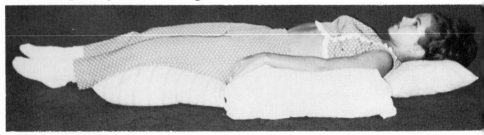

Figure 9-12. A pillow under both knees will relax muscles and relieve tension.

If you sleep on your side, bend your knees and hips so that your thighs and legs are flexed nearly to right angles. Then put a pillow between your knees to keep your upper thigh from sagging down.

IMPORTANT: When you sleep on your back, don't use such a thick pillow under your head that your chin is tilted toward your chest. It's important to keep your neck in line with the rest of your spine when you're sleeping.

STRETCHING YOUR SPINE TO RELIEVE BACK AND LEG PAIN

A long day of sitting and standing very often results in backache caused by compression of joints and discs. And if the spine has been weakened or deformed by arthritic spurs or degenerated discs, leg pain may result from compression of delicate nerves.

Persons who are sway-backed are especially susceptible to compression-type backache and leg pain.

If you develop a bone-like ache, numbness, or tingling in one of your legs for no apparent reason, you may be suffering from nerve irritation that can be relieved by stretching your lower spine.

How to Stretch Your Spine Without Expensive Equipment

There are four simple exercises that you can do to relieve aches and pains caused by compression of your spine. Any one of them may provide complete relief. Select the exercise that is most convenient for you and try it first. If it doesn't relieve your pain, try the next exercise. If none of the exercises seem to help, or if your pain persists or grows worse, see your doctor.

1.   ROLL UP INTO A KNEE-CHEST BALL: Lie on your side and pull your knees up toward your chest. Let your lower back round out so that the joints on the back of your spine will spread apart to relieve pressure on joints and nerves. (See Figure 9-13.)

Figure 9-13. Sway-back backache can be relieved by pulling both knees to the chest.

Don't do this exercise forcefully. Try to roll up into a ball, but don't strain. Stop the minute you feel any pain or discomfort.

I frequently recommend this exercise for sway-backed persons who suffer from backache caused by prolonged standing. A sales clerk, for example, can slip into a back room and do the exercise whenever he has a rest break.

2. TRACTION WITH A CHAIR: Lie on your back on the floor and drape your legs over the arm of a heavy sofa. The support of the chair arm beneath your knees should be just high enough to lift your hips from the floor. You may have to place a couple of pillows between your legs and the chair arm to get the lift you need. (See Figure 9-14.)

Figure 9-14. Resting with the legs draped over the arm of a sofa will ease low-back and leg pain.

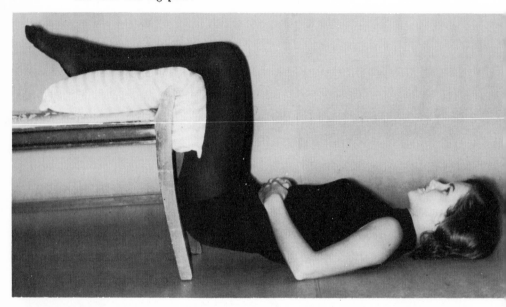

Try to lie relaxed in this position for several minutes or until your back and leg pains have eased. This is a relaxing posture that anyone can use for relieving backache. Overworked housewives, especially, should use this chair traction technique several times a day.

3. FROG KICK ON A CHINNING BAR: Hang from a chinning bar or a tree limb and lift both knees up toward your chest so that your lower back is rounded out. Then lower your legs and hang relaxed for a few seconds. (See Figure 9-15.)

Figure 9-15. The "frog kick" will stretch muscles and expand discs.

The frog kick will stretch and align your spine to relieve pressure on joints, discs, and nerves. It will also stretch the muscles of your back.

This is an excellent exercise for backache-plagued factory workers who must stand around on concrete floors all day.

4. TRACTION BETWEEN TWO CHAIRS: If you work in an office and you don't have access to a horizontal bar, you can get a good traction by suspending your weight between two chairs.

Slide the chairs close together and stand between them. Place one hand on each chair and support your weight on your locked-out arms. With a little practice, you can relax the muscles of your back enough to feel your lower spine stretch under the weight of your lower body. Let your feet rest on the floor, but don't support any weight with your legs. (See Figure 9-16.)

A 68-year-old retired business executive who had suffered a compression fracture in his spine many months earlier was able to relieve his backache as well as his leg pain with this traction technique when conventional traction failed.

*Figure 9-16. Supporting your weight be-
tween two chairs will relieve nerve pressure
in the lumbar spine by stretching the lower
back.*

A SPECIAL EXERCISE TO UNLOCK YOUR SPINE

If you develop a backache or back pain that seems to "lock" your spine, and none of the other traction exercises seem to help, a simple exercise that rotates your vertebrae might do the trick.

A Back-Rotating Exercise

Lie on your back with your trunk, thighs, and legs flexed at right angles to each other, as though you were sitting in an overturned chair. Hold your legs in this "sitting position" and drop them first to one side and then to the other by twisting at your waist. Keep your shoulders and upper back flat on the floor. Place your arms alongside your body with your palms pressing against the floor for counterbalance. Do several repetitions in each direction. (See Figure 9-17.)

This exercise is designed primarily to unlock your lower back.

A Simple Technique for Adjusting Your Upper Back

Roll up a sheet of rubber or rug padding and secure it with a couple of pieces of heavy string. Place the roll on the floor and then lie down on the roll so that it crosses the middle of your upper back. Place your hands behind

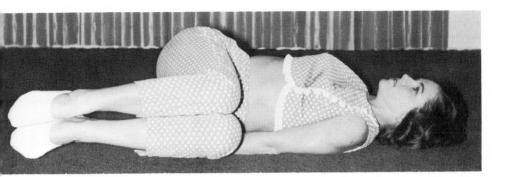

Figure 9-17. You can unlock "kinks" in your lower back by rotating your spine while lying down.

your head and then lower your head to the rug and relax. The pressure of the roll will straighten your upper spine and "adjust" your vertebrae. You may occasionally hear a "pop" in your back as a result of movement in the joints. (See Figure 9-18.)

Figure 9-18. "Kinks" in your upper back can be relieved by lying back over a roll of rubber or carpet padding.

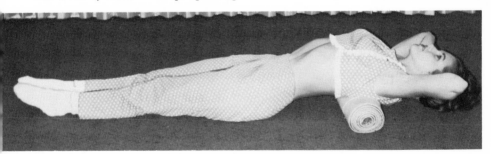

This is a fine "manipulation" for persons who suffer from the binding fatigue of prolonged postural strain.

A COMPLETE BOOK ON BACKACHE

If you suffer from chronic backache, you'll want to read my book *Backache: Home Treatment and Prevention*, available from your local book store or from Parker Publishing Company (West Nyack, New York 10994). It covers all aspects of backache, and it's designed for use by the layman who wants to treat his back at home.

SUMMARY

1. Always face the object you intend to lift and then lift with your legs instead of with your back.

2. Basically, good standing posture means standing tall with your chest up, your abdomen flat, and your toes pointed nearly straight ahead.

3. Whenever you sit in a straight-back chair, sit erect with your buttocks against the chair-back and a slight hollow in your lower back.

4. If you have backache after performing physical work, you can relieve your symptoms with rest, moist heat, and massage. But if your backache is the result of prolonged sitting or standing, your symptoms would best be relieved with exercise.

5. If you have a job in which you must sit most of the day, you should take special exercises (described in this chapter) to prevent shortening of your hip flexors and hamstrings.

6. Your mattress should be firm enough to prevent your spine from sagging, but not so hard that it cannot mold itself to the normal curves of your body.

7. When you have a backache, a pillow under both knees may relieve tense muscles while you are lying on your back.

8. Lying down with your legs draped over the arm of a sofa, or suspending your weight from a chinning bar or between two chairs, may relieve leg pain by stretching your lower spine.

9. Tighten the "guy wires" supporting your spine by taking a little regular exercise for your abdominal and back muscles.

10

Improve Your Health
with Foot and Leg Care

If you went to a doctor for treatment for a headache and he examined your feet, you might wonder if he knew what he was doing or if he was just "pulling your leg." Actually, it's not at all uncommon for foot trouble to trigger aches and pains in other portions of the body.

No one completely escapes the occasional discomfort of aching feet. Most people suffer from "bad feet." One reason for this is that practically everyone now wears heavy, overly supporting shoes that weaken the muscles of the feet. Whenever the shoes are improperly fitted—as they almost always are—abnormal pressures on the feet distort muscles, bones, and ligaments to cause all kinds of crippling foot trouble.

HOW BAD FEET CAN AFFECT YOUR WHOLE BODY

Mrs. M.S., a 43-year-old super-market cashier, complained of low-back, hip, and knee pain. She had been to many doctors, with no results, and none had ever looked at her feet. When I asked her if her feet ever hurt, she said "Sure they hurt, but not nearly as bad as my back and legs. If I could just get rid of this backache, I could put up with my foot trouble."

It hadn't occurred to Mrs. M.S. that she might have unbalanced feet that could be throwing the rest of her body out of balance. What was happening was this: Her arches were so weak that they could not withstand the leverage of lifting her heels from the floor when she walked. Years of wearing high-heeled shoes had also shortened her ankle tendons. As a result, she had developed a slew-footed stance in order to relieve the strain on her arches and to reduce the pull on her ankle tendons.

Whenever she stood during work, a rolling in of her ankles rotated her knees inward so that her pelvis tilted forward to produce a sway back. This was causing backache as well as leg ache.

In addition, the tension of the muscles up and down her spine was so great that she nearly always had a tension headache at the and of the day.

All of her aches and pains were relieved with a single exercise, a change in foot posture, and properly fitted shoes.

Just about everyone has some of the same type of foot trouble that Mrs. M.S. had. Look at your own feet. Do they point outward when you walk? Do your ankles roll inward when you stand? This chapter will tell you everything you need to know to build strong, healthy feet.

HOW TO PROTECT YOUR FEET FROM UNACCUSTOMED STRAIN

Try to avoid subjecting your feet to an excessive amount of unaccustomed work—such as standing or walking all day, as in visiting a fair or marching in a parade. Running or carrying heavy loads can also strain the feet.

You should try to exercise your feet, but you should begin lightly and then slowly increase the amount of exercise you do over a long period of time. If you're accustomed to wearing shoes most of the day, don't work or run without them. Walking barefoot in the sand is a good exercise for the feet, but don't overdo it at first.

WHY IS THE FOOT SO VULNERABLE TO STRAIN?

If you've ever seen an X-ray of the foot, you know that it looks like a loosely constructed bridge that's liable to collapse at any moment. (See Figure 10-1.)

Figure 10-1. Without the support of strong muscles and ligaments, the bones of the foot would collapse.

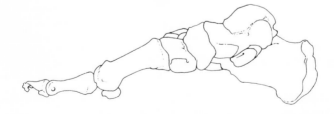

There are 26 movable bones in the foot, and they are held together entirely by muscles and ligaments. When the muscles have been weakened by lack of exercise and too much shoe support, the bones sag against the ligaments during walking and standing. If the ligaments are strained by an overload, the feet may hurt for many hours after they're relieved of weight bearing.

Occasionally, displacement of bones in the feet will pinch nerves and obstruct the circulation of blood to cause many strange pains and sensations that defy diagnosis.

POOR CIRCULATION AS A CAUSE OF FOOT TROUBLE

If you are past middle age, poor circulation may be a factor in the production of your foot trouble. The feet are so far away from the heart that blood circulates slowly and sometimes inadequately. Tightly fitted leather shoes may also press the thin layers of flesh against the bones to cause corns and calluses from an almost complete lack of circulation.

If the circulation in your feet and legs is poor, you may have to wear thick socks to keep your feet warm when you are sleeping. If you suffer from foot and leg cramps, you may also have to get up at night to exercise your feet in order to stimulate the flow of blood.

The most serious complication of poor circulation in the feet is the slow healing of burns and injuries. For this reason, you should make a special effort to take care of your feet and to avoid such unnecessary irritations as improperly fitted shoes.

Hardened arteries are a common cause of poor circulation. Turn back to Chapter 5 and study it carefully.

THE COMPLICATION OF DIABETES

If you have diabetes, you must make an *extra* special effort to avoid foot injuries. A high blood sugar along with poor circulation may permit a blister or a small cut to develop into an ulcer or a festering wound that heals very slowly.

Don't Apply Heat to Diabetic Feet

A burn can be a very serious injury for a diabetic. You shouldn't apply a hot-water bottle or a heating pad to your feet if you have a high blood sugar level. Be careful not to let your feet get sunburned when you go wading at the beach.

Keep Your Feet Covered

When you're working in the yard or in a shop, always wear leather shoes rather than slippers or sandals in order to protect your feet from injury. If you should suffer a cut or bruise, see your doctor immediately.

MAKE SURE YOUR SHOES FIT

Probably the most important thing to remember in buying a pair of shoes is this: *Make sure the shoes fit your feet rather than force your feet to fit your shoes.*

As a rule, the shoe should be about one-half inch longer than the longest toe. A shoe that is too short or too narrow to allow for expansion of the foot during walking and standing can literally squeeze the life out of your feet. Jamming together the bones in the forepart of the foot can pinch nerves, push joints out of alignment, and injure the lubricating sacs that surround the joints.

Are Arch Supports Really Necessary?

If you don't have bad feet or weak arches, you shouldn't buy shoes with built-in arch supports. The inside of the shoe should, whenever possible, conform to the shape of the bottom of the foot. However, no effort should be made to lift up a normal arch.

A sponge rubber pad under the instep of your foot will provide just enough support to remind you to maintain good foot posture. Shoe support should not completely relieve the work of the muscles that maintain the arch.

When the feet are constantly supported by rigid arch supports, the muscles and ligaments are weakened from lack of use. Then, when they are suddenly subjected to unaccustomed strain, the arches may "give way" or fall to cause crippling foot pain.

If you have strong, normal feet, it's all right to wear tennis shoes occasionally if you observe the rules of good foot posture. In fact, it is a good idea to go barefoot every chance you get. But whenever you're doing a lot of standing or walking, you should wear a good leather shoe that has a thick sole and a rigid shank. (The shank is the portion of the shoe between the heel and the front sole.)

How to Test the Shank of a New Shoe

Place the shoe on the floor and press down against the portion of the shoe that supports the arch of the foot. If the shank bends, the shoe is cheaply constructed and is not rigid enough to keep a weak arch from sagging.

Breaking in a New Pair of Shoes

Whenever you buy a new pair of shoes, wear them for only a few hours each day until you've broken them in. Don't throw away your old shoes until you can wear your new shoes comfortably all day. This means that you shouldn't wait until your shoes are completely worn out before buying a new pair.

HOW TO AVOID OBSTRUCTING THE FLOW OF BLOOD TO YOUR LEGS

You already know that the circulation of blood through the feet is less than anywhere else in the body. Don't reduce it even more by obstructing the flow of blood through your legs.

Observe the rules of correct sitting posture (Chapter 9) so that you won't be placing any pressure on the big blood vessels on the back of your legs. The "pins and needles" in your feet are almost always caused by pressure on nerves and arteries.

Don't ever sit for very long with your legs crossed. Jamming of the supporting knee into the back of the draped-over leg may cause a temporary partial paralysis by damaging important nerves, making if difficult to lift your toes when you walk or run.

Beware of Tight Garters

Elastic garters or hose may also interfere with the circulation of blood to your feet and legs. And if you have varicose veins, worsening of the condition may cause your feet to swell.

If you have knee trouble, be careful not to wrap the knee too tightly with elastic bandages. If you do wear such supports, take them off whenever you aren't on your feet and then lie down so that the blood can flow through your feet and legs without any interference from gravity. (Chapter 13 describes simple techniques that you can use to drain stagnant blood out of your legs.)

A SPECIAL NOTE ABOUT HIGH HEELS

I've learned in my many years of practice that it's futile to try to talk the average woman out of wearing dressy shoes with pointed toes and high heels. Few women want to be *"out of fashion,"* regardless of the consequences. I must admit that in many cases a pair of lovely legs are indeed enhanced by the sloping, tapered shoes that have become a symbol of femininity.

The fact remains, however, that the typical female's shoe is a torture chamber for the foot. Prolonged use of such shoes will invariably cause foot trouble. The down-hill slope of high-heeled shoes literally jams all five toes into the narrow, pointed portion of the shoe. This causes corns, calluses, bunions, and ingrowing toe nails.

If you must wear shoes with high heels and pointed toes, wear them only on special occasions—when you want to "dress up" for only a few hours. *Try to avoid wearing shoes with heels over two inches high.* Select a shoe that's wide enough in front to accommodate your toes without forcing them to overlap each other.

WHAT CAUSES BUNIONS?

The bunion, which is characterized by a build-up of bone and callus at the base of the big toe, is very often complicated by partial dislocation of the toe joint. In most cases, this is caused by pointed shoes that squeeze the toes together.

ANKLE TENDONS AND HIGH HEELS

If you've been wearing high-heeled shoes most of your life, your ankle tendons have probably shortened a great deal. For this reason, you shouldn't suddenly switch from high heels to low heels. Lower your heels gradually and stretch your ankle tendons with the heel-stretching exercise described in this chapter.

Whenever the heels are dropped too much too soon, a pull transmitted through tight ankle tendons and hamstrings may cause backache by pulling on the pelvis. Also, there may be a tendency to walk with the toes pointed outward to lessen the tension on the back of the legs. This can lead to a rolling inward of the ankles and knees to cause both back and leg pain—like that experienced by Mrs. M.S., the super-market cashier.

So while you shouldn't wear extremely high heels, it's entirely possible that you'll get along better with a little heel than with no heel at all.

We spend two-thirds of our life in shoes, and most of us walk enough to go from coast to coast each year. If you wear badly fitted shoes, your feet will never make it—and you won't either.

WHAT TO DO ABOUT CORNS AND CALLUSES

If you wear properly fitted shoes, chances are you won't develop corns and calluses. If you are afflicted with these disorders, let a chiropodist trim them for you. Persons who attempt to whittle down their own corns with a pocket knife or a razor blade nearly always cut too deeply.

After the dead tissue has been removed, you can use an emery board to file down any additional build-up. It's important to remember, however, that corns and calluses will recur if the circulation is obstructed by pressure. If the pressure and irritation can be removed by changing shoes, the build-up of dead tissue will eventually disappear.

THE IMPORTANCE OF EXERCISE

The ligaments that bind the bones of the foot together are the first line of defense in maintaining the arch of the foot. Once these ligaments have been stretched or injured, the muscles won't be able to maintain the arch. For this reason, you should make a special effort to strengthen the muscles of the foot so that the ligaments won't be forced to assume more than their share of the load. With a little extra muscle protection, the arch of the foot will be strong as well as flexible.

There are about 20 muscles in the foot, but the three that support the arch under the inside portion of the foot are the most important. Here are three exercises that you can do to strengthen weak arches, correct bad foot posture, and stretch ankle tendons.

1. Heel Raises

Stand with the forepart of your feet on the top surface of a thick board or a step. Point your feet inward (in a pigeon-toed direction) and rise up and down on your toes. Lower your heels as far as you can in order to stretch your ankle tendons. (See Figure 10-2.)

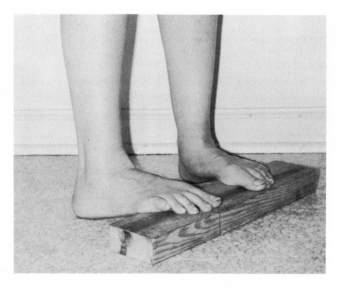

Figure 10-2. *Women who wear high heel shoes should stretch their ankle tendons by doing heel raises from a 2 × 4.*

Begin by doing only a few repetitions and then progressively increase the number you do over a period of several days. Too much stretching the first few days can result in painfully sore calf muscles. Work up to about 20 repetitions.

After you become accustomed to this exercise, you can place an even greater stretch on your ankle tendons by doing your heel raises while leaning over with your legs locked out straight and your hands braced on a low bench.

NOTE: Always remember to place a board—preferably a 2×4—under the forepart of your feet when doing heel raises. Rising up and down on your toes on the floor would only increase the shortness of ankle tendons and cause further toeing out and rolling in of the ankles.

Testing for Tight Ankle Tendons

You can test the tightness of your ankle tendons with this simple exercise.

Sit in a chair and lock your leg out straight in front. Then lift your foot up toward your shin by bending only your ankle. If you can't lift the forepart of your foot up past a 90 degree angle—that is, past a right angle to your shin—your ankle tendons are much too short. (See Figure 10-3.)

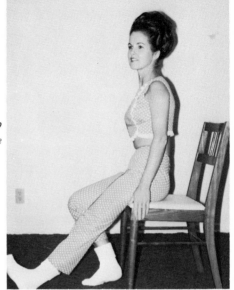

Figure 10-3. If you cannot lift your foot up past a right angle to your shin, your ankle tendons are too short.

2. Resistive Foot Flexion

One of the muscles on the front of the lower leg passes down under the inside of the foot to form a sling for the arch. Since this muscle functions in *lifting* the foot, it will be necessary to lift the foot against resistance in order to build maximum arch strength.

Sit on the edge of a high table so that your legs will dangle without your feet touching the floor. Hang a weight, such as a handbag filled with sand, over the top of your foot and lift it up and down with ankle action only. Try to use enough weight to tire your shin muscles in 12 to 15 repetitions. (See Figure 10-4.)

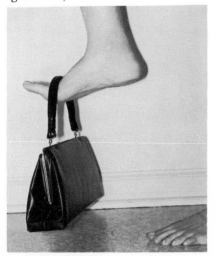

Figure 10-4. An important muscle supporting the arch of the foot can be strengthened by lifting the forepart of the foot against resistance.

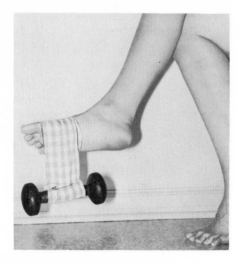

Figure 10-5. Turning the foot inward against resistance is also a good arch-strengthening exercise.

3. Resistive Foot Adduction

Next attach a weight to the shoe so that it hangs from the big-toe side of your foot. You can do this by tying a long strip of cloth to the weight and then wrapping the free end around the forepart of your foot so that the weight is suspended near the big toe. With your leg dangling, curl your foot inward, with ankle action only, as though you were trying to look at the bottom of your foot. (See Figure 10-5.)

Use a weight that's heavy enough to fatigue your foot muscles in 12 to 15 repetitions.

HOW TO ASSUME GOOD FOOT POSTURE

Foot posture in its relationship to overall posture was discussed in Chapter 9. Because of the importance of good foot posture in protecting the feet, however, there are certain basic rules that are worth repeating in this chapter.

Basic Rules of Good Foot Posture

Stand and walk with your toes pointed nearly straight ahead. Lift your arches up a little so that your weight is supported on the outside edges of the soles of your feet. Don't let your ankles roll toward each other to flatten your arches on the floor. (See Figure 10-6.)

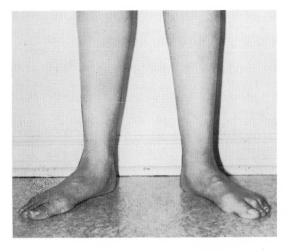

Figure 10-6. In bad foot posture, the feet are pointed outward and the arches are flattened against the floor.

It'll take a little practice to maintain good foot posture without thinking about it. If you can develop the habit of keeping your toes pointed nearly straight ahead, chances are you'll also hold your arches up. (See Figure 10-7.)

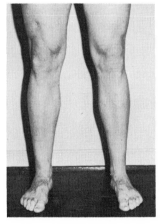

Figure 10-7. In good foot posture, the weight is supported on the outside edges of the soles of the feet and the toes are pointed nearly straight ahead.

Try to keep your ankles centered over your feet so that your center of balance falls between the first and second toe of each foot. This will automatically distribute your weight on the balls of your feet.

USING SOLE WEDGES

If you find it difficult or impossible to maintain good foot posture, a chiropodist might be able to help by altering your shoes. If you are slew-footed, for example, a small leather wedge inserted up and down the big-toe side of each shoe sole will force your feet to point inward rather than outward. Persons who are pigeon-toed, however, should have the wedges attached to the little-toe side of each shoe sole.

HOW TO MANIPULATE YOUR FEET

Because of the tendency of the average person's feet to point outward and his ankles to roll inward, most of us can benefit from the same basic manipulative technique.

Arch Manipulation

Sit in a chair and cross over the leg of the foot you want to manipulate. Grasp the top, forepart of the foot with one hand and then encircle the arch with the thumb and forefinger of the other hand. Twist and turn the foot up toward your face while pressing against the arch. (See Figure 10-8.)

Figure 10-8. Foot manipulation after a day of standing or walking can provide welcome relief for aching feet.

This simple manipulation will reverse the strain that's placed on the arch during weight bearing, and it's perfectly safe for anyone to use. Whenever your feet ache after a day of walking or standing, slip off your shoes, wherever you may be, and manipulate each foot several times.

A postman who delivers his mail by walking told me that he manipulates his feet each evening when he gets home. "My feet don't hurt nearly as much as they used to," he said. "I wouldn't take anything for that foot treatment you told me about."

I recommended the same treatment to Betty H., a department store employee who was on the verge of quitting her job because of "bad feet." The treatment enabled her to keep her job. "Sometimes I get a sharp, burning foot pain that shoots up my leg like a hot poker," she said. "Every time this happens, I pull off my shoe right there in the store and manipulate my foot. It always relieves the pain." Betty's pain was being caused by a pinched nerve, which could be released by adjusting the bones of her foot.

A Special Big-Toe Manipulation

If you wear shoes with pointed toes, you should also manipulate your big toe by stretching it while pulling it away from the rest of the toes. This will help prevent the misalignment that causes severe bunions. (See Figure 10-9.)

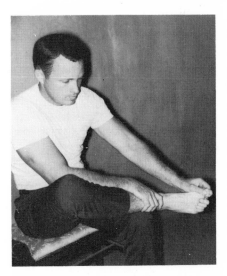

Figure 10-9. A special big-toe manipulation can prevent bunions and maintain alignment of metatarsal bones.

A thin felt or rubber pad between the big toe and the first toe will help keep the big toe joint aligned. The end of the shoe must be round rather than pointed, however, to provide enough room for both the toes and the pad.

IMPROVE CIRCULATION WITH A CONTRAST BATH

Since the circulation of blood is usually very poor in the feet of persons past middle age, fatigue and aches and pains in the feet can sometimes be relieved by stimulating the flow of blood with alternate hot and cold foot baths. The cold will squeeze blood out of the feet by contracting the blood vessels, while the heat will flush the feet with blood by dilating the blood vessels.

Technique of Contrast Bath

Get two deep tubs and fill one with hot water (100 to 110 degrees Fahrenheit). Immerse your feet and legs in hot water for four minutes and then in the cold water for one minute.

Alternate the hot and cold immersions for a total of five immersions, beginning with hot and ending with cold.

WATCH FOR SWELLING AROUND YOUR FEET AND ANKLES

If your feet and ankles swell from poor circulation, you can reduce the swelling simply by lying down and elevating your feet. But if your ankles are puffy and water logged, you may need specialized medical care.

Testing for Edema

Press your thumb against the portion of the foot or ankle that appears to be swollen. Maintain the pressure for several seconds. If a deep impression remains in your flesh when you remove your thumb, you have edema, which can be caused by any one of a variety of disorders. Restrict your salt intake until you can be examined by a doctor. Don't apply hot or cold applications to your feet unless he advises you to do so.

OTHER CAUSES OF FOOT PAIN

There are many things that can cause pain in the foot. Bony spurs, calcium deposits, gout, arthritis, tumors, and so on, may require specific treatment that only a chiropodist or orthopedic specialist can prescribe.

If you wear properly fitted shoes, practice good foot posture, and take your exercise, along with any other self-help measure that might be indicated, you'll be able to prevent or relieve most forms of foot trouble. Whenever a foot pain persists or grows worse, call your doctor for an appointment.

GOOD FOOT HYGIENE IS ALSO IMPORTANT

Perspiration is a big factor in the development of skin trouble around the feet. It's well known that fungus and bacteria thrive on moist, soft skin. "Athlete's foot," for example, is very common among persons who wear airtight leather shoes for long hours each day.

Try to wear white cotton socks that are thick enough to absorb plenty of moisture. Thin nylon socks tend to bottle up your feet in their own perspiration.

Dust your feet (especially your toes) with a good medicated powder each time you take a bath or before your put on your shoes. This will relieve itching by absorbing moisture and restricting the growth of fungus.

During the summer, wear a perforated shoe that will permit air to circulate around your feet.

SUMMARY

1. Improperly fitted shoes, bad foot posture, and lack of exercise are the most common causes of foot trouble.

2. Bad foot posture causes mechanical imbalances that can cause leg, hip, and back pain, as well as nervous tension and headache.

3. Always buy shoes that are about one-half inch longer than your longest toe. Remember to fit the shoe to your foot rather than force your foot to fit your shoe.

4. If you do a lot of standing or walking, wear a good leather shoe that has a thick sole and a rigid shank.

5. Don't buy shoes with built-in arch supports unless your doctor prescribes them.

6. Always stand and walk with your toes pointed straight ahead. Lift up your arches slightly so that your weight is supported on the outside edges of the soles of your feet.

7. Stretch your ankle tendons and strengthen the muscles of your feet by rising up and down on your toes from the edge of a thick board.

8. You can stimulate the flow of blood in your feet by immersing them first in hot water and then in cold water for several immersions.

9. If you have diabetes, don't apply heat to your feet.

11

Stop Needless Suffering
from Hernia

Charlie B. was once a champion tennis player. When he retired from athletics, he quit exercising completely and accepted a sales position with a sporting goods company. Several years later he began to experience a little soreness and swelling in his right groin.

"You have an inguinal hernia," the doctor told him. "If that bulge gets any bigger, it may have to be repaired surgically."

Charlie was flabbergasted. "How could I have a hernia?" he asked. "I've been an athlete most of my life, and I haven't done anything to strain myself."

Bonnie J., a housewife and a mother, developed a groin hernia after the birth of her second child. The doctor told her that she had a "femoral hernia."

"I thought only men had hernias in that part of the body," she said. "What's the difference between a femoral hernia and an inguinal hernia? What can I do about it?"

Like most people, Charlie and Bonnie had no idea what a hernia was or how it occurred. Both of them might have been able to prevent their hernia if they had observed certain precautions. Luckily, both were able to "cure" their hernia by doing the simple exercises described in this chapter.

WHAT YOU CAN DO ABOUT HERNIA

Although hernia occurs most often in persons who are born with abdominal defects, it can be prevented if a special effort is made to avoid abdominal pressures and to strengthen the abdominal muscles.

When hernia does occur, it can sometimes be controlled with special exercises if they are started *before* the herniation is complete.

Until a hernia actually develops, it may be difficult for your doctor to tell whether or not you might be a potential victim of hernia. So even if you do not now have a hernia, *you should observe the simple rules and safeguards outlined in this chapter in order to make sure that you do not develop a hernia.*

MOST HERNIAS OCCUR IN THE LOWER ABDOMEN

Hernia can occur in many places in the body, especially around the abdomen, but it's most common in the *lower* abdomen. The reason for this is that there are openings in this portion of the abdominal wall where certain structures pass down into other portions of the body. Both males and females have these openings, but a difference in the size of one of the openings makes the male more susceptible to hernia.

INGUINAL HERNIA MOST COMMON IN THE MALE

The inguinal opening near the pubic bone serves as a passageway for the spermatic cord in the male and a ligament in the female. Since there is a larger opening in the male than in the female, the male is more subject to inguinal hernia. In fact, about four-fifths of all hernias are inguinal hernias, and most of them occur in men.

Hernia may occur through a normal inguinal ring when it is subjected to severe pressures, but it occurs more readily through a ring that has been weakened by a birth defect. In some cases, hernia is unavoidable. Most of the time, however, it can be prevented by building up the muscles that surround the opening.

FEMORAL HERNIA IN THE FEMALE

The femoral opening provides a gateway for the large nerves and blood vessels that supply the thighs and legs. While femoral hernia occurs in both males and females, it is more common in females. Persons who are born with unusually large femoral rings are most susceptible to femoral hernia.

WHAT HAPPENS WHEN HERNIA OCCURS?

Normally, the femoral and inguinal rings fit snugly about the structures passing through them. Whenever the rings are too large, or if they are stretched by excessive abdominal pressures, the intestinal tract and the lining of the abdominal wall push through to form a bulge just beneath the skin.

If the bulge is near the pubic bone and is above the ligament that separates the thigh from the abdomen, your doctor will call it an "inguinal hernia." If it's higher up in the groin and is below the inguinal ligament, it will be called a "femoral hernia."

Advanced Hernia

In the early stages of either type of hernia, there's only a slight bulging over the femoral or inguinal ring. It may even be difficult to tell what type of hernia it is. As the hernia becomes more complete, however, it will follow the course of the structures that normally pass through the opening. In inguinal hernia in the male, for example, the bulging intestinal tract may drop down into the sac (scrotum) that houses the testicles. When this happens, surgery is the only remedy.

Inguinal hernia in the female may bulge into the major labia (the outer tissues surrounding the entrance to the vagina).

In femoral hernia in both males and females, the bulging intestinal tract follows the course of the blood vessels down into the thigh.

The Danger of Bowel Strangulation

The greatest danger of hernia is strangulation of the protruding bowel. A loop of intestine becomes so twisted or pinched off that it develops gangrene from lack of adequate blood supply. This is a very serious condition that must be corrected immediately by surgery. If you develop fever and other symptoms of illness along with a painful hernia, call your doctor.

In many cases, a hernia can be pushed back through the abdominal opening by lying down and manipulating it with the fingers. A truss (a belt with a pad that fits over the opening) may then be worn to keep the intestine from falling back through. This should never be done when it proves to be painful, however, or if there is reason to believe that the bowel is twisted.

THE PROTECTION OF A LEAN ABDOMEN

Many persons who are born with structural defects in their abdominal wall will not develop hernia as long as their waistline is kept lean and trim with exercise. The reason for this, as explained in anatomy books, is that the thicker the muscles and tendons that surround the inguinal and femoral rings, the greater the protection against hernia. Fortunately, *the layers of muscle in the lower abdomen can be made thicker as well as stronger with special exercises.*

In the case of Charlie B., who developed a hernia for no apparent reason after retiring from athletics, it was not strain or injury that led to hernia. He developed the disorder because his soft, sagging abdominal muscles could no longer keep his intestinal tract from tumbling down to the bottom of his abdomen.

Charlie was born with a weak inguinal ring, but as long as he exercised he had the protection he needed to prevent hernia. As he grew fatter and flabbier from sedentary living, however, the weight of his fat-ridden abdominal organs and the pull of gravity were enough to stretch the inguinal opening so that a loop of intestine could bulge through. Lack of exercise had allowed the muscles surrounding the opening to shrink, leaving it unguarded and vulnerable.

HOW CHARLIE B. CURED HIS HERNIA

I instructed Charlie in the corrective exercises described in this chapter, put him on a diet, and then told him to avoid the strains and pressures that contribute to hernia. After several months on this program, there was no longer any bulging in his groin. He still had the structural defect in his abdominal wall, but the size of the opening had been considerably reduced. He eliminated excessive abdominal pressures by practicing the breathing technique described later in this chapter.

Bonnie J. was also able to reduce her hernia by following the same program.

Both Charlie and Bonnie are now active, lean, and happy, and they're no longer worried about submitting to surgery that would be costly in both time and money.

EARLY EXERCISE IS BETTER THAN LATE SURGERY

Many hernias recur after they have been repaired surgically. Whenever the muscles surrounding an inguinal ring are weak and thin, and the abdomen is fat and flabby, there's little to prevent the weakened tissues from once again tearing or stretching. For this reason, it's always best to first try exercise in correcting a hernia. Then, if the bulge becomes larger in spite of all you do, you can submit to surgery if your doctor advises it. Your well-developed abdominal muscles will contribute to a faster and more permanent recovery from the surgery itself.

The older you become, the more important it is to keep your abdominal muscles lean and strong if you want to prevent hernia. So don't quit exercising just because you're "retired." Regular abdominal exercises will make you feel better and look better.

The simple exercises described in this chapter will require only a few minutes of your time. You don't have to do them more often than every other day.

SELECTING THE EXERCISES YOU NEED

If you don't have a hernia, you may do the resistive exercises that are designed to prevent hernia. If you already have a hernia, however, you should do the two special exercises.

Hernia is easier to prevent than to cure. If you do develop a hernia, remember that it must be corrected *before* the herniation is complete; otherwise, surgery may be necessary.

CAUTION: If any of the exercises seem to aggravate your hernia, discontinue them.

THREE RESISTIVE EXERCISES TO PREVENT HERNIA

Do all three of these exercises to make sure that the muscles and tendons on both sides of your abdomen are thick and strong.

1.   Bent-Knee Sit-Ups on an Incline Board

If you've never done sit-up exercises, you should first do them on the floor in order to become accustomed to them. Then, as you grow stronger, you may do them from an incline board (with your feet anchored at the high end of the board) for greater resistance. By progressively increasing the incline of the board, you can increase the resistance of the exercise as well as the thickness of your abdominal muscles with only 10 to 15 repetitions.

Occasionally do your sit-ups with a twist so that you touch your right elbow to your left knee in one repetition and your left elbow to your right knee in the next repetition. This will exercise the muscles in the groin area more specifically. (See Figure 11-1.)

Be sure to *curl* your upper body up from the board so that your abdominal muscles rather than your hip flexors will do most of the work. Always *exhale* during each sit-up.

Don't worry about making your waistline larger by developing your abdominal muscles. Although these muscles do get a little thicker when exercised against resistance, they do not develop like muscles in other portions of the body. An overweight waistline will become smaller as the abdominal muscles grow stronger.

Figure 11-1. *Twisting sit-ups on an incline board are effective for building protection against hernia.*

2. Leg Raises on the Floor

You should also do leg raises in order to strengthen the hip flexors for additional protection against hernia. (Leg raises help reinforce the femoral ring, while sit-ups reinforce both the femoral and inguinal rings.)

Begin by doing the exercise with your knees slightly bent. (See Figure 11-2.)

Lie on your back with your arms alongside your body and raise both legs while holding them in a bent position. Don't raise them any higher than straight up and down. As you grow stronger, gradually straighten out your legs for greater resistance.

Do eight to ten repetitions. *Exhale* while you raise your legs.

NOTE: Discontinue sit-ups and leg raises if they seem to hurt your back. The leverage and the pull of the hip flexors on the lower spine will sometimes aggravate a "bad back." You can, however, do the two "special" exercises in the next group.

Figure 11-2. *Bent-knee leg raises will strengthen the muscles of the lower abdomen without straining a weak femoral or inguinal ring.*

Figure 11-3. Side bends with a dumbbell will build additional protection against hernia.

3. Side Bends with a Dumbbell

Stand erect with a weight or a dumbbell in one hand and bend from the side for several repetitions. Exercise both sides equally. (See Figure 11-3.)

Side bends will strengthen the muscles that run obliquely down the abdomen on each side to form the inguinal ligament. Development of these muscles will build maximum protection against hernia.

TWO SPECIAL EXERCISES TO REDUCE A HERNIA

If you already have a hernia and it isn't past the stage of a slight bulge, you may be able to reduce it permanently by taking these two exercises.

1. Trunk Curls on an Incline Board

Lie down on a steeply inclined board with your feet anchored at the high end of the board. Put your hands behind your head and curl only your head and shoulders up from the board. This will strengthen the abdominal muscles without activating your hip flexors and without placing too much pressure on the lower abdomen. Also, gravity will pull the intestinal tract away from the abdominal rings while the abdominal muscles are contracting. (See Figure 11-4.)

As you grow stronger, you may hold a bag of sand against your chest for greater resistance in eight to ten repetitions. *Exhale* each time you contract your abdominal muscles.

HELP YOUR HERNIA BY RELAXING ON AN INCLINE BOARD: Simply lying relaxed with your head at the low end of an incline board will permit

162

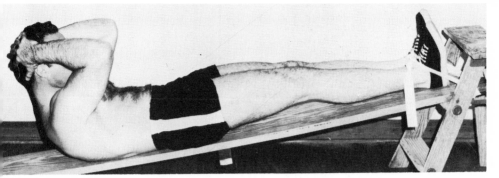

Figure 11-4. Once hernia occurs, trunk curls on an incline board may be used to rebuild abdominal strength.

the intestinal tract and the abdominal organs to roll back and reduce the pressure in the lower abdomen. Inhale deeply and lift your chest up high for a diaphragm suction effect that will literally pull your abdominal organs out of the pelvic bowl.

SWITCHING TO SIT-UPS: When there is no longer any bulging in your groin, you may bend your knees and do regular sit-ups. Begin lightly and cautiously, however, and remember to exhale while sitting up.

2. Leg Raises on an Incline Board

Nail a strip of wood across the bottom side of the board so that it will project out on each side as handles. You should be able to grip the handles at about hip level while you're lying on the board.

Prop one end of the board up on a low, sturdy box. With your head at the low end of the board and your hands gripping the handles, raise your legs up while holding your knees in a bent position. Don't get careless and let your legs fall back over your head to jackknife your body. *Exhale* during each repetition. (See Figure 11-5.)

HOW TO BREATHE TO PREVENT HERNIA

How you breathe while you're exercising or working can be very important. You should *never* take a deep breath and hold it during an exertion. When you inhale, your diaphragm moves downward to place a little pressure on your abdominal organs. If you hold a deep breath by closing the muscles of your throat, and then tighten your abdominal muscles during a heavy effort, you'll place a terrific compression on your abdominal organs. This could push your intestinal tract right through a weak or enlarged femoral or inguinal ring.

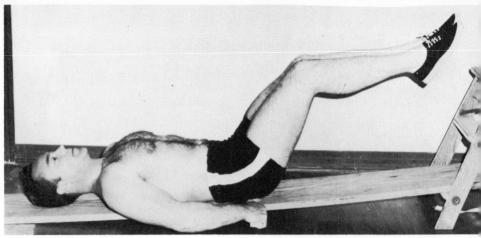

Figure 11-5. Decline bent-knee leg raises can be used to exercise the lower abdomen without placing pressure on a hernia.

Rupture may even occur through a normal ring if the pressure is heavy enough.

IMPORTANT: Memorize this crucial rule of breathing. *Always exhale during an exertion.* Leave your glottis (throat) open so that exhalation will automatically take place whenever contraction of the muscles around your chest and abdomen compresses the rib cage or the abdomen.

HOW HERNIA CAN OCCUR WITHOUT PAIN

Since most hernias occur gradually over a long period of time, simple, everyday strains may lead to hernia without any obvious pain or soreness. Without any warning whatsoever, you suddenly discover that you have a tender swelling in your groin. In such cases, the weight of the abdominal organs and the pull of gravity may be responsible for pushing the intestinal tract through a weak and underexercised abdominal ring.

Many people do not discover that they have a hernia until a heavy exertion causes pain by stretching the already damaged tissues. Be sure to take your exercises and to observe the rules of correct breathing, whether you think you have a hernia or not.

THE PAIN OF ACUTE HERNIA

If you should rupture a normal abdominal wall while holding your breath during an exertion, the sudden tearing or stretching of healthy tissue will result in severe pain that is associated with shock, nausea, and other symptoms of illness. The thin tissue that lines and seals the abdominal cavity is very sensitive. Whenever it is suddenly ballooned out through a stretched inguinal or femoral ring, the victim experiences great pain.

Bed Rest for Acute Hernia

In many cases, an acute hernia will reduce itself with bed rest. Special exercises may then be used to tighten up the abdominal muscles to prevent a recurrence of the hernia under normal conditions.

SUMMARY

1. Most hernias occur in persons who are born with defects in the rings or openings normally found in the wall of the lower abdomen.

2. Although hernia is sometimes unavoidable, the disorder can be prevented in most cases by taking special exercises to keep the abdomen lean and flat.

3. A hernia can very often be reduced with bed rest or by lying down and manipulating the protruding intestine back through the opening.

4. Hernias that aren't "complete" can be permanently reduced by taking special exercises that will strengthen and thicken the muscles surrounding the abdominal rings without increasing the pressure in the lower abdomen.

5. Don't ever take a deep breath and hold it during an exercise or an exertion. Always *exhale* when you contract your abdominal muscles.

6. Avoid postures that place compression on the contents of the abdomen. For example, be careful not to sneeze while you're tying your shoe.

7. Turn back to Chapter 9 and review the correct lifting techniques. You can "rupture" yourself as well as strain your back when you lift improperly.

8. Most hernias are of the inguinal type, and most of these occur in the male. Femoral hernia occurs primarily in the female.

9. Don't do any exercise that increases pain or swelling in your groin.

10. The older you become, the more important it is to take regular abdominal exercises in guarding against hernia.

Eat for Youthful Health and Strength

"You are what you eat," a college instructor told his class on dietetics.

A student raised his hand for permission to speak. "I know a man who eats nothing but chicken. How come he doesn't look like a chicken?"

Of course, the student was only trying to be funny. He knew very well what the instructor was trying to say. Many people might ask such a question, however. Most of us know that there must be adequate amounts of protein, carbohydrate, fat, water, vitamins, and minerals for the body to be strong and healthy, but too few of us really know *how* to eat.

EAT TO REMAIN PHYSICALLY ATTRACTIVE

It would be misleading to say that good eating habits will make you prettier or more handsome, but it is true that your physical appearance depends largely upon what you eat. Deficiencies in any one of the numerous food elements that are known to be essential for best health, for example, can lead to changes in the skin, eyes, nails, or hair. Even a person's attitude can be affected. It's now well known that vitamin deficiency is a major cause of "nervous conditions" and mental illness.

An unhealthy person with a sallow skin, bags under his eyes, and a miserable countenance can hardly go around looking radiant and energetic. Nothing can shatter an individual's image or aura more than a mouth full of decaying teeth. Skin that's marred with splotches and eruptions certainly isn't appealing to look at or touch. Bones softened by a mineral deficiency can bend and sag to distort the beauty and symmetry of the body. There are many ways in which your body will reflect bad or unwise eating habits.

None of these things need to happen. You can prevent them or eliminate them by exercising a little control over what you eat.

THE WARNING OF POOR HEALTH

Many of the vague complaints of poor health are the forerunners of worse things to come. Don't ignore them.

You already know from reading Chapter 5 that eating too much animal fat may contribute to death from heart disease by clogging the arteries with fatty sludge. Many health problems result from an accumulation of chemicals that the body absorbs from excessive use of artificial foods.

Of all the causes of disease and poor health, improper eating would undoubtedly be near the top of the list. There are, however, certain simple rules and guidelines that anyone can follow in making sure that the body is adequately nourished. Study this chapter carefully and then help yourself by eating as others have done. Don't wait until poor health warns you of possible disaster.

EXAMPLES OF SELF-HELP CORRECTIVE EATING

An overweight secretary addicted to pastries and sweets complained of chronic fatigue. "I thought sweets were supposed to give you energy," she said, "but the more I eat the worse I feel." You'll learn in this chapter how artificial sweets can deplete your body of energy-giving Vitamin B.

A young attorney relieved his recurring muscle spasms by drinking a pint of milk each day. Two periods of hospitalization and one year of exercise had not helped a bit. When he added milk to his diet, his trouble vanished. The "secret" of milk is yours for the reading in this chapter.

A 73-year-old retired railroad executive restored strength to his softened bones by supplementing his diet with bone meal. One vertebra in his weak and brittle spine had already collapsed. Had he not changed his eating habits, his entire spine would have eventually become deformed by a chain of compressed and distorted vertebrae.

An overworked housewife who suffered from headaches, hives, and crying spells was able to relieve her symptoms by supplementing her diet with nerve-building yeast tablets. "I've even quit taking tranquilizers," she said, "and I feel like a new woman." A formerly unsuccessful insurance salesman cured his anemia, restored his initiative, and got back in the "race" simply by eating a couple of dried liver tablets each day.

Whatever your trouble might be, there may be a food or a concentrated food supplement that will erase your symptoms and restore your capacity to enjoy living. Don't be a failure simply because you don't eat correctly.

Eating is a pleasure. You can get more out of life and the foods you eat if you eat good foods rather than bad foods.

THE SEVEN BASIC FOOD GROUPS

If you want to be assured of getting adequate vitamins and minerals from wholesome foods, divide your foods into the seven basic food groups and then eat at least one food from each group every day.

The seven basic food groups are: (1) Green and yellow vegetables; (2) Citrus fruit, tomatoes, raw cabbage; (3) Potatoes and other vegetables and fruits; (4) Milk and milk products, such as cheese; (5) Meat, poultry, fish, eggs, dried peas, beans; (6) Whole grain or enriched bread, flour, and cereals; (7) Butter and fortified margarine.

You don't have to eat great volumes of these foods to be healthy. Your body needs only small amounts of the various vitamins and minerals, but it needs them all in balanced amounts. *It's much better to eat small amounts of a great variety of foods than to eat large amounts of only a few foods.*

NATURAL FOODS ARE BEST

Whenever possible, eat fresh, natural foods rather than canned or refined foods. For example, you should learn to prefer brown rice rather than white rice, pure whole wheat bread rather than white bread, fresh greens rather than canned greens, and so on. The skins of fruits and vegetables, when edible, are very rich in vitamins and minerals.

Don't ever buy fruit "drinks" rather than fruit juice, or candy rather than dried fruit. Whenever you're buying the groceries, first ask yourself: "Is this a natural food?" Then ask yourself: "Is it fresh?"

You Need Those Undiscovered Vitamins

If you find it impossible to eat a balanced and wholesome meal each day, it may be a good idea to include a multiple vitamin supplement. It's important to remember, however, that fresh, natural foods contain many yet undiscovered vitamins, enzymes, and other substances that are not found in pills containing isolated vitamins and minerals.

For this reason, you cannot depend upon vitamin pills alone for complete nourishment. Even if you do take food supplements, you should still make a special effort to eat at least one balanced meal each day.

Don't forget that your body needs protein, carbohydrate, fat, and other elements along with vitamins if it is to function normally. It's much better to
get these from wholesome, tasty foods than to try to stock your medicine
cabinet with bottles containing everything your body needs.

A glass of milk, an orange, and a piece of cheese have much more to offer
your body and your taste buds than a hit and miss collection of pills and powders.

You Can't Live on Empty Calories

Don't worry about getting fat eating natural foods (see Chapter 5). Just
about everyone I know who is overweight eats white bread, pastries, candy,
soft drinks, and other refined and synthetic foods that contain "empty calories." Since such foods do not supply the body with adequate vitamins and
minerals, they do not satisfy the appetite. As a result, the individual eats excessive amounts of high-calorie foods that do little more than build up fat
stores.

SPECIAL DIETS FOR SPECIAL CASES

If your diet must be altered in some way because of illness, injury, or
pregnancy, let your doctor prescribe a specific food supplement for you. In
this way, you can put back into your diet the food elements that may be missing and that you know you need.

Persons who are on an ulcer diet, which usually consists of milk, cream,
cereals, and eggs, may need Vitamin C. Babies and children who satisfy their
appetite with milk may need additional amounts of Vitamins C and D. People
who eliminate fat in a reducing diet or because of gall bladder trouble may
need Vitamin A. Alcoholics almost always need massive doses of Vitamin
B. Various intestinal disorders that interfere with absorption and utilization
of certain vitamins may need a special combination of vitamins and minerals,
and so on.

Vitamins as Therapy

It's all right to supplement your diet with pills and powders when it's simply a matter of improper eating. When a deficiency exists because of disease
or illness, however, or vice versa, vitamins and minerals must be prescribed

in therapeutic doses by a doctor. This means that in some cases vitamins must be injected into the body.

Study the deficiency symptoms and the sources of the vitamins and minerals listed in this chapter and then make a special effort to get more of the foods supplying the food elements you think you need.

Each vitamin has many functions in the body, and all of them work together in maintaining health. Practically all of the vitamins and minerals we know about can be found in varying amounts in almost everything we eat. However, only the major deficiency symptoms and the important food sources will be mentioned in this chapter.

HOW TO GET ALL YOUR VITAMINS AND MINERALS

So far, medical scientists have uncovered about 20 vitamins that are believed to be essential to human health. If you make a special effort to eat foods that are known to be rich in several of the better known vitamins and minerals, you'll get everything else your body needs in adequate amounts.

The body of an animal can manufacture the vitamins it needs from whatever type of food it eats, but we humans must seek a wide variety of foods in order to get the nourishment we need.

Eating for better health and a longer life cannot be left to chance or instinct. You must be knowledgeable about the foods you eat, and you must eat scientifically.

VITAMIN A FOR YOUR EYES AND SKIN

If you have trouble seeing at night, or if you have any kind of chronic infection or skin disorder, you may not be getting enough Vitamin A.

A 19-year-old college girl who had been on a reducing diet for several months cleared up her respiratory infection as well as her complexion by eating liver a couple of times each week.

The skin and membranes covering your body and its cavities provide your first line of defense against infection. Keep them healthy by eating foods rich in Vitamin A.

Sources of Vitamin A

The richest sources of Vitamin A are found in foods of animal origin—

whole milk, butter, cream, cheese made from whole milk, egg yolk, liver, and fish liver oils. *Liver is the richest of these sources.*

The carotenes of plant pigments that are found in yellow vegetables (papaya, carrots, squash, yellow corn, cantaloupes, sweet potatoes) and in the dark green leaves of vegetables (turnips, spinach, lettuce, collards) can be broken down in the liver and converted to Vitamin A.

SPECIAL VITAMIN A SUPPLEMENTS: If you eat a balanced diet, you'll include foods rich in Vitamin A. If you're on a low-fat diet, however, you should make a special effort to eat more yellow and green fruits and vegetables. *Nonfattening fish liver oil is rich in Vitamin A, and it's low in saturated fat.*

Since your liver can store Vitamin A, undesirable side effects can result from taking too many high-powered Vitamin A capsules. If your doctor prescribes this vitamin in concentrated form, be careful not to take more than recommended on the label.

A SKIN BONUS: Basically, the appearance of your skin depends upon proper nutrition. But if you want a beauty treatment that will soften and tone your skin, try this oil bath. Rub soya oil or olive oil into your skin and then scrape it off with a plastic or rubber spatula. This will clean clogged pores and remove dead skin.

VITAMIN B₁ FOR STEADY NERVES

Have you been suffering from nervousness, fatigue, depression, irritability, insomnia, constipation, loss of sleep, and poor appetite? If so, you might need a little extra B_1 or thiamine.

In addition to feeding the nerves, thiamine helps your body convert sugars and starches into fuel for energy. A deficiency may result in a tired, listless feeling that is difficult to overcome.

A nervous salesman who complained that he was always tired but couldn't sleep at night reported that he felt "rejuvenated" after increasing his intake of thiamine. His apathy and pessimism disappeared and his sales zoomed.

Food Sources of Vitamin B₁

Most meats are rich in Vitamin B_1, but *pork and ham are by far the richest.* If you do eat pork, make sure that it's well cooked in order to eliminate any chances of infection by a type of worm that can invade your muscles and your vertebrae (trichinosis). Don't ever eat pork that has a pink color.

Whole grain cereals and bread, wheat germ, peas, beans, and soybeans are also good sources of thiamine.

SPECIAL B_1 SUPPLEMENT: If you don't eat much meat, *mix powdered brewer's yeast in milk or fruit juice* for Vitamin B insurance. Yeast contains 17 different vitamins, including all the B vitamins. It's also rich in protein and minerals, and it contains only one percent fat.

PREVENT PREMATURE AGING WITH VITAMIN B_2

If you eat meat, fish, poultry, eggs, green leafy vegetables, and whole wheat bread, you'll probably get adequate amounts of Vitamin B_2 (also called ribo-flavin). But if you seem to be aging prematurely, or if your eyes are sensitive to light and there are sores or cracks at the corners of your mouth, you should include food yeast, broiled liver, wheat germ, and milk in your diet in order to make sure that you're getting more than adequate amounts of the B vitamins. Food yeast can be purchased in a variety of tasty flavors for between-meal snacks.

One of my patients, an 84-year-old boat builder who is still plying his trade, believes that his strength and energy come from eating whole wheat bread, which he makes himself. "White bread is nothing but pasty cake," he said. "I never eat it."

VITAMIN B_6 FOR HEALTHY TEETH

If you're deficient in one B vitamin, you may be deficient in others. A deficiency in any one of them may cause similar symptoms. Recent research, however, has indicated that a shortage of Vitamin B_6 (also called pyridoxin) in the diet may contribute to tooth decay and hardening of the arteries.

PREVENT ANEMIA WITH VITAMIN B_{12}

We all know that an iron deficiency can cause anemia, but many people do not know that a deficiency of Vitamin B_{12} can also cause anemia (as well as disease of the nervous system).

This vitamin is commonly found in liver, salt water fish, and other foods of animal origin. Certain stomach and intestinal disorders, however, may prevent absorption of B_{12}. When this happens, it may be necessary for your physician to prescribe a special therapeutic supplement to replace an "intrinsic" substance normally produced in the stomach. This is one reason why anemia should be treated by a physician.

Since Vitamin B_{12} is not present in fruits and vegetables, vegetarians should include some milk and animal products—or fish—in their diet.

OTHER B VITAMINS

There are several other vitamins that belong in the B group. Some of these are folic acid, pantothenic acid, niacin (also called nicotinic acid), choline, inositol, and biotin.

If you eat a variety of foods of animal and vegetable origin, you'll get all these lesser known B vitamins. A deficiency of one or a combination of them can result in nervous, gastrointestinal, and skin symptoms. A deficiency of niacin, for example, is a common cause of pellagra among people who do not eat meat and vegetables.

ALL TOGETHER: B COMPLEX

Since all the B vitamins work together in maintaining health, they are usually grouped together and called "Vitamin B Complex." To make sure that you get all these vitamins, add these foods to a balanced diet: (1) broiled beef or calf liver at least once a week; (2) a tablespoonful of powdered food yeast in a glass of milk or fruit juice each day; (3) wheat germ sprinkled over cereals and salads each day.

When you can get it, use fresh wheat germ rather than the toasted variety you find on grocery store shelves.

If you think your diet might be deficient in B vitamins in spite of what you eat, ask your druggist for a bottle of Vitamin B complex. A doctor's prescription won't be necessary.

Why You Might Be Deficient in Vitamin B

Too many Americans literally live off soft drinks and refined and artificial foods. In addition to being deficient in vitamins, such foods contain concentrated sugar and starch that "burn up" the Vitamin B supplied by other foods.

Removal of the outer germ layers of grains in milling or processing strips them of vitamins. Since Vitamin B is needed in the metabolism of the starchy portion of the grain, excessive use of white flour and the other refined grain products tends to divert B vitamins from the nervous system to the metabolic fires.

Synthetic B vitamins are now being added to bread and other white flour products. It's important to remember, however, that whole grain products probably contain undetected food elements that may be essential for best health.

You Need Vitamin B Every Day

Unfortunately, the body doesn't store Vitamin B beyond its immediate needs. This means that you must supply your body with B vitamins *each day*. If you take in more than your body can use, your kidneys will simply excrete the excess.

Whenever you find it impossible to get away from the coke and sandwich circuit, take along a little food yeast for a supplementary snack. Your health food store can supply you with tablets that you can carry around in your pocket.

Seeds and Nuts Are Rich in Vitamins

Most seeds and nuts contain B vitamins, especially B_6. Peanuts, pecans, almonds, walnuts, sunflower seeds, and pumpkin seeds, for example, make delicious and nourishing between-meal snacks—and they're low in saturated fat and high in unsaturated fat. You know from reading Chapter 5 that unsaturated fat (along with certain B vitamins) tends to prevent hardening or collection of fat in the arteries.

VITAMIN C FOR QUICK HEALING OF INJURIES

You already know from reading Chapter 8 that Vitamin C (also called ascorbic acid) builds resistance against colds and infections. It also reduces bleeding and speeds healing of wounds. A deficiency results in scurvy, a disease characterized by swollen and bleeding gums.

Many athletes take Vitamin C tablets in order to strengthen tissue cells and capillaries so that bruises won't be made worse by excessive bleeding in the tissues. Most of them report that their injuries are less severe and their recovery more rapid.

Sources of Vitamin C

Your body does not store Vitamin C, so you must make a special effort to get adequate amounts of this vitamin *each day* to remain in the best of health. You can do this easily by eating citrus fruits. Broccoli, strawberries, tomatoes, cabbage, and greens are also good sources of Vitamin C. Try to eat some of these foods every day. A handful of fresh strawberries will provide you with a full day's supply of ascorbic acid.

Rose hips are also rich in Vitamin C. Your health food store will have this product already prepared for consumption. (A rose hip is the portion of the rose bud that remains after the petals have fallen.)

If you smoke, you need more Vitamin C than the average person. Research has shown that nicotine destroys this vitamin in the blood. If you want to quit smoking, try substituting licorice sticks for cigarettes until you can break the habit.

Since Vitamin C is easily destroyed by heat, light, air, oxygen, and other factors, foods containing this vitamin should be fresh, natural, and raw whenever possible.

You can't get too much Vitamin C. Be cautious, however, about drinking quart after quart of fruit or vegetable juice each day, as some people do on a "juice diet." The acid in these juices may erode the lining of your stomach.

KEEP YOUR BONES STRONG WITH VITAMIN D

Bone-building Vitamin D is free! All you have to do is to let the sunlight bathe your skin, and your body will manufacture this vitamin. The ultraviolet rays will convert an oily substance on the skin to Vitamin D, which is then absorbed by the body.

Expose as much of your body as you can to the sun's rays, but don't overdo it. Too much sun will age the skin prematurely and give it a wrinkled, leather-like appearance. Expose yourself gradually to avoid sunburn. Then limit your exposures to just enough time to maintain a light tan. Efforts to maintain a dark tan thoughout the year may contribute to the development of skin cancer.

Whenever there is not an adequate amount of Vitamin D in the body, calcium and phosphorus cannot be utilized effectively in building good teeth and strong bones. In adults, the bones may soften enough (osteoporosis and osteomalacia) to permit some of the vertebrae to collapse like crushed egg shells.

Lack of exercise is also a cause of bone softening in older people. Those who cease all physical activity when they "retire" can expect both their bones and muscles to soften.

Sources of Vitamin D

Enriched milk and fish and liver oil are the best food sources of Vitamin D. Fish and egg yolk also contain fair amounts of this vitamin.

SPECIAL SUPPLEMENTS: If you work at night and sleep during the day, or if you spend most of your time indoors, you should add a little *fish liver oil* to your diet. Exposing your salad oils and cooking oils to sunlight will increase their Vitamin D content. Just pour the oil into a flat pan and expose it to the sun's rays for at least two hours.

CAUTION: Like Vitamin A, Vitamin D can be stored in the body. Excessive amounts of this vitamin in the form of pills and capsules can upset your body's utilization of calcium and other minerals. If your doctor prescribes a high-powered Vitamin D supplement for medicinal purposes, don't take any more than he recommends. Don't ever give a child an adult's dose.

VITAMIN E FOR A HEALTHY HEART MUSCLE

Although very little is known about Vitamin E, there are many medical scientists who maintain that it is essential for a smoothly functioning heart. It also aids the body in building strong red blood cells that aren't easily damaged in their circulation through the body.

Research has indicated that persons who are on a low-cholesterol diet need increased amounts of Vitamin E to prevent oxidation of important unsaturated fatty acids (and Vitamin A).

Many athletes maintain that the Vitamin E found in wheat germ oil gives their muscles more strength and stamina. It may do the same for you. Since it is high in unsaturated fatty acids, it will lower your blood cholesterol rather than raise it.

Sources of Vitamin E

Cereal and plant oils, such as wheat germ oil, corn oil, cotton seed oil, and soybean oil, are rich in Vitamin E and low in saturated fat. Vegetable margarine (specially treated to retain unsaturated fat), eggs, meats, butter, whole grain cereals, lettuce, nuts, and seeds of all types also contain Vitamin E.

Unprocessed or raw wheat germ is an inexpensive and tasty source of Vitamin E. Just mix it with other foods, such as cereal, salads, bread, and meat loaf.

Other whole-grain products, such as graham flour, brown rice, dark rye flour, and corn meal also retain their outer vitamin-rich germ layers.

Vitamin E in Reproduction

Ancient Greeks believed that lettuce was an aphrodisiac (sex stimulant). Today, we know that lettuce is rich in Vitamin E, which is believed to be essential in reproduction.

VIRILITY BONUS: Sarsaparilla tea contains hormone-like (testosterone) substances that stimulate the male sex glands. Ask your health food store for sarsaparilla tea bags.

Pumpkin seeds (purchased unshelled) also contain ingredients that boost male hormones. If you're past 40 and going "downhill," try snacking on sarsaparilla tea and pumpkin seeds.

Powders, tea, and other products made from licorice (an extract from the roots of a European plant) are believed to have a stimulating effect on female estrogenic hormones.

SPECIAL VITAMIN E SUPPLEMENT: Raw wheat germ or a couple of tablespoons of wheat germ oil each day will give you the Vitamin E insurance you need.

VITAMIN K FOR NORMAL CLOTTING OF BLOOD

Vitamin K is widely distributed in nature. It can even be manufactured by the bacteria in our intestines. This is fortunate for us, since it plays an important role in the clotting of blood. Without it, we would bleed for hours from the smallest cut.

Sources of Vitamin K

Just to make sure that you get adequate amounts of Vitamin K, eat plenty of green leafy vegetables. Liver, egg yolk, and soybean oil are also good sources.

VITAMINS MUST BE ACCOMPANIED BY MINERALS

If you get your vitamins from fresh, natural foods, you'll automatically get most of the essential minerals. Check your diet periodically, however, to make sure you include foods rich in calcium, iron, and iodine. Foods containing these three minerals also contain all the other minerals.

Like vitamins, minerals are important for the function and the integrity of every cell in the body. A deficiency of any one of these elements may be compared with the proverbial "weak link" in the chain. To be completely healthy, you must have a balanced intake of *all* the vitamins and minerals.

CALCIUM FOR BONES, TEETH, NERVES, AND MUSCLES

Calcium is needed in relatively large amounts to build and maintain healthy teeth and bones. It also aids in the clotting of blood and in the conduction of nerve impulses to muscles. Even the contraction of the heart muscle depends upon the presence of calcium in the blood.

Muscle Spasm Caused by Calcium Deficiency

One of the most common symptoms of early calcium deficiency is nervous irritability and muscle spasm.

If you suffer from painful leg and foot cramps, especially at night, you may be able to eliminate your trouble simply by increasing your intake of calcium-rich foods.

Sources of Calcium

Milk is the best source of calcium for the average person. In fact, some nutritionists maintain that it's difficult for the average adult to get enough calcium without drinking a pint of milk each day.

Don't mix chocolate with your milk. This may result in a chemical reaction that will prevent absorption of some of the calcium.

Naturally sweet carob powder may be used to give milk a delicious chocolate taste—and it's rich in minerals. Stir in a little molasses and yeast for a "nerve drink" that's rich in both calcium and Vitamin B. You can enrich your milk even more by adding a little powdered skim milk, mixed to suit your taste.

If you don't like milk, try to eat milk products, such as cheese, yogurt, buttermilk, homemade ice cream, and so on. Powdered milk may be added in generous amounts to homemade bread, custards and other foods in order to raise their protein and calcium content.

Green leafy vegetables are fairly rich in calcium—with the exception of spinach, beet greens, and sorrel, which contain an acid that may prevent utilization of the calcium.

SPECIAL SUPPLEMENTS: Remember that your diet must also contain Vitamin D and phosphorus in order for your body to use calcium. If you have any doubt about your diet containing all these elements in balanced amounts, supplement at least one meal each day with *bone meal* or *powdered egg shells.* Try mixing a little bone meal in a glass of milk.

If you have an ulcer and you're on a milk diet, be cautious about using commercial antacids. Combining milk and alkali may create an excess amount of calcium in your blood, which may then be deposited in the soft tissues of your body.

A NOTE ABOUT YOUR TEETH: There are some nutritionists who maintain that teeth won't decay if the diet is rich in calcium, phosphorus, Vitamin D, and Vitamin B_6, along with other essential vitamins and minerals. You should, however, brush your teeth after each meal and each night before retiring. Whenever food particles remain in the teeth overnight, increased bacterial action tends to erode the enamel.

BUILDING RICH, RED BLOOD WITH IRON

About 70 percent of all the iron in the body is formed in the red blood cells where it's called "hemoglobin." Whenever there is a deficiency of iron, the body becomes anemic, and the ability of the blood cells to transport oxygen is impaired.

One of the first symptoms of iron deficiency—and anemia—is fatigue and lack of pep. Advanced symptoms include such things as soreness of the mouth and tongue, pallor, tingling of the hands and feet, and so on.

Since stomach acid is essential for the absorption of iron, don't take soda or alkalizers more often than necessary.

Sources of Iron

Iron is found in many foods, but liver and dark green vegetables are our best sources. Dried fruits, such as raisins, are also rich in iron. They may be eaten between meals to supply energy and to curb the appetite, or they may be eaten as desserts following meals.

SPECIAL SUPPLEMENT: If you want added assurance that you're getting plenty of iron, supplement your diet with desiccated liver (tablets or powder) or dark molasses.

If you need a little extra iron-rich energy in the middle of a hard work day, mix a small amount of brewer's yeast and molasses in a glass of grape juice.

IODINE FOR WEIGHT CONTROL AND IMPROVED THINKING

Persons who are overweight and sluggish, or underweight and nervous, are often victims of "thyroid trouble." The thyroid gland in the neck may even enlarge to form a goiter. In severe cases, lack of thyroid hormones may slow reflexes and impair thinking.

All this can be prevented in most cases by making sure that the diet contains adequate iodine.

Sources of Iodine

Vegetables grown in iodine-rich soil can supply limited amounts of this important mineral. If you live in the region of the Great Lakes or the Rocky Mountains where the soil is deficient in iodine, you'll have to make a special effort to eat iodine-rich foods.

Seafood is rich in iodine. *Try to eat seafood at least once a week.* Broccoli is also a good source.

Fortunately, most commercial table salt now contains iodine. For this reason, goiter is not very common these days. Other symptoms, however, such as dry skin and brittle hair and nails, are fairly common.

If you do develop a goiter, it must be treated by a physician. But if you show any indications of subclinical iodine deficiency, you can help yourself by eating iodine-rich foods.

SPECIAL SUPPLEMENT: If you don't eat fish, you should supplement your diet with *dried kelp*. It's rich in iodine, and it can be purchased very cheaply in powder or tablet form in any health food store.

The sea is rich in minerals, and provides nourishing "soil" for the growth of kelp and other forms of plant life.

HOW TO GET THE MOST OUT OF THE FOOD YOU EAT

It's not enough to know which foods are rich in certain vitamins and minerals. If a food cannot be eaten in a fresh, natural state, it must be properly prepared if it is to retain the elements that are essential to health.

Always Select Fresh Foods

Whenever possible, select foods that you know are fresh. Most foods lose some of their vitamins when there is a long delay in getting them from their source to your dinner table. A freshly picked orange, for example, has more Vitamin C than an orange that has been on the market for several days. Milk stored in glass containers loses some of its Vitamin B to sunlight.

Exposure of almost any fresh food to air, light, changes in temperature, and other factors tends to destroy the delicate vitamins and enzymes.

If you're not sure how fresh a food is, observe its color, smell, and texture. A frozen chicken that has a bad odor, a piece of meat that has changed colors, fruit that's dry and wrinkled, a vegetable that's limp and spongy—all these things point to stale, vitamin-depleted foods.

IMPROPER COOKING IS THE GREATEST KILLER OF VITAMINS

The average cook destroys many of the vitamins in the food he prepares by cooking them too long at too high a temperature. Boiling foods in water, or submerging them in cooking grease, also destroys vitamins.

HOW TO SAVE WATER-SOLUBLE VITAMINS

Vitamins B and C are known as "water-soluble vitamins." This means that they go into solution in the presence of water. Whenever foods are cooked by submerging them in water, some of these vitamins are literally washed from the food into the water. Then, if you throw away the water, you throw away the vitamins; that is, those that aren't destroyed by the high temperature. The longer you cook the food, the more vitamins you lose to heat and water.

You should always try to broil your meats. Vegetables should be cooked with as little water as possible for as short a cooking time as possible.

Cooking Technique

Select a heavy cooking container that's just big enough to hold the vegetables you want to cook. Use a waterless, stainless steel pot if you have one. Such pots usually have heavy, overlapping lids that will hold in the steam.

Put a small amount of water in the pot—a cup or less—and heat it until it begins to steam. Then put in the cut vegetables, place the lid on the pot, and cook at as low a temperature as possible and still keep the water steaming.

The less air that circulates in the pot the better. Keep the lid on tight and shake the pot occasionally to shift the positions of the cooking vegetables. The steam does all the cooking.

DON'T OVERCOOK: Don't cook your vegetables any longer than necessary to soften them. Cooking them until they fall apart or until they become mush will destroy much of their food value.

With a little practice, you can learn just how much water you must use in the bottom of the pot to get the vegetables cooked in the shortest possible time. Too little water increases cooking time, while too much water dissolves vitamins.

BOILING VEGETABLES: If you must boil some of your vegetables, first heat the water to boiling and then put in the vegetables. This will stop the boiling temporarily, but you may turn the heat up a little in order to start the water boiling again. The flames should then be reduced just low enough to keep the water boiling.

USING THE COOKING WATER: If you have any water left in the pot after boiling your vegetables, use it to make soups or broths. Or you may boil it down to make a sauce that can be poured over the cooked vegetables.

KEEP COOKED VEGETABLES COVERED: Vegetables should be served as soon after cooking as possible. If they are allowed to stand for very long after cooking, they will lose some of their vitamins to oxidation. This is one reason why you shouldn't depend upon cafeteria lunches for your vitamins.

Always keep your vegetables covered so that oxygen won't steal their vitamins.

COOK ONLY AS MUCH AS YOU CAN EAT IN ONE DAY: Reheating leftover vegetables is a bad practice. Some restaurants actually cook vegetables over and over—or they heat them before each serving by pouring hot water over them. Such repeated heating and washing leaves only a small part of a vegetable's original food value.

To be sure that the vegetables you eat are nourishing, cook them fresh each day. Don't cook so much that you have leftovers for tomorrow's dinner.

If you must eat in restaurants every day, try to supplement your diet with the natural food supplements mentioned earlier in this chapter.

HOW TO SAVE FAT-SOLUBLE VITAMINS

Vitamins A, D, E, and K are found in fatty foods and are best absorbed in the presence of fat. But when foods containing these vitamins are cooked in an excessive amount of grease, the vitamins may be lost in the pan or in undigested cooking grease.

When any one of the water-soluble or fat-soluble vitamins is lost in cooking, it becomes more difficult for your body to make use of the other vitamins and minerals. You already know, for example, that Vitamins C and D facilitate the absorption and use of calcium.

Use as little grease as possible in cooking. Whenever you have a choice, select foods that have been baked or broiled rather than boiled or fried in cooking grease.

COOK MEAT AND VEGETABLES SEPARATELY: Even if you don't cook your meats in grease or oil, you know that all meats contain fat. For this reason, you should cook your meats and vegetables separately so that the vegetables won't soak up the meat drippings. A grease-soaked potato or carrot is neither healthy nor tasty.

Bake or broil your meat on a split grille so that the cooked-out grease will fall through into a bottom pan.

BEWARE OF FRIED FOODS

You learned in Chapter 5 that the high fat content of fried foods may be fattening, if not bad for your heart and your arteries. If you do fry foods occasionally, don't ever heat the grease to such a high temperature that it begins to smoke. Overheated grease breaks down chemically to form a poisonous substance that irritates the digestive tract and places a burden on the body's metabolism.

Why You Should Use Vegetable Oil in Frying

Lard and other animal fats (containing saturated fat) tend to smoke at a lower temperature than vegetable oils (which contain unsaturated fat). So for your stomach's sake, as well as for your heart's sake, you should use vegetable oil (except olive oil) in deep-fat frying.

Each time a fat is reheated in frying, its smoking temperature becomes lower. This means that using the same grease over and over will result in a progressive deterioration of its fatty acids. I learned this fact the hard way back in my college days when I used the same bacon grease several times to fry potatoes. I became very ill with a gastrointestinal upset that was finally traced to my cooking grease.

I don't eat much fried food these days; but when I do, I instruct the cook to use fresh vegetable oil.

NOTE: Although vegetable oil withstands heat better than animal fat, you should not depend upon fried foods for your unsaturated fatty acids. Heat destroys lecithin and other important anti-cholesterol factors in the oil. Cold-pressed vegetable oil or fresh vegetables are your best sources of unsaturated fat. Be sure to read Chapter 5.

How to Fry Your Foods

When frying, always heat your grease before dropping in the food. This will quickly cook the outer surface of the food so that it won't soak up grease during the actual cooking.

When cooking has been completed, remove the food from the pan immediately and place it on absorbent paper towels. There is no excuse for serving fried foods that shine with grease. Only the worst kind of cook would serve fried foods that drip with grease when they are squeezed.

Unfortunately, there are some cooks who believe that a food is too dry without a little clinging grease. Many of them are not at all averse to letting fried foods soak in a pan of grease before serving them.

WHAT ABOUT FROZEN FOODS?

If you have a choice, you should always select fresh foods. When these aren't available, frozen foods are the next best choice. If they have been properly packaged and frozen, they'll contain just about as many vitamins and minerals as fresh foods. A food that has been kept frozen for too long a period of time, however, may lose some of its vitamins.

How to Pick Frozen Foods

Buy your frozen foods at a busy super market where frequent restocking is required. Always pick clean packages that are sealed and unsoiled. Don't buy frozen foods that are covered with frost or that have broken or loose wrappers. Ice indicates that the food may have been thawed and then refrozen. Whenever air gets between the food and its wrapper, precious vitamins are lost to light and oxygen. Circulating air also activates enzymes and bacteria that lead to spoilage and a change in flavor.

Frozen foods should never be allowed to thaw until just before they're eaten or cooked. If you have a freezer, keep your foods frozen frost-free at 0 degrees Fahrenheit. If shopping facilities are convenient, don't buy more than one week's food supply at a time.

CANNED FOODS: YOUR THIRD CHOICE

Whenever a food item is not available in fresh or frozen form, it may be taken from a can in order to balance a meal. Today's canned goods retain most of their vitamins and minerals, and they are generally quite wholesome. Many of them, however, contain chemical preservatives.

Even canned foods lose some of their vitamins when they are stored for a long period of time, so don't depend upon them for complete nutrition.

AVOID SYNTHETIC FOODS

If you don't remember anything else from reading this chapter, at least remember to make fresh, natural foods your first choice in eating. This single guideline will do more for your health than any other measure, and it will add years to your life.

You may save a little money by buying artificial, preserved or refined foods, but you may pay dearly with minutes and hours of your life. Refined foods may be deficient in some of the elements you need to build and maintain health, while preserved or artificial foods may contain chemicals that will accumulate in your body to cause disturbing side effects.

SUMMARY

1. The first rule of good nutrition is to eat natural foods that are *fresh*— and they should be eaten raw whenever possible.

2. Each time you eat, select at least one food from each of these four food groups: milk and cheese; meat, poultry, fish, and eggs; fruits and vegetables; whole grain bread and cereals.

3. Study the vitamin-deficiency symptoms and the food sources listed in this chapter and then adjust your diet accordingly.

4. If you want to supplement your diet with concentrated natural foods, consider using food yeast, powdered skim milk, bone meal, desiccated liver, wheat germ, fish liver oil, dried kelp, and sun-dried fruit.

5. Remember that excessive use of sugars and starches will produce fatigue by robbing your body of Vitamin B and overstimulating the production of insulin.

6. If you make sure that the food you eat contains adequate amounts of calcium, iron, and iodine, you'll automatically get adequate amounts of the other minerals.

7. Use as little water as possible for as short a cooking time as possible when preparing a meal.

8. Serve foods as soon after cooking as possible, and keep them covered to prevent exposure to circulating air.

9. Vitamins and enzymes are very sensitive to heat, light, air, and other factors. Some of them can be washed or dissolved out of foods when they are cooked in water or oil.

10. Don't heat cooking grease until it smokes. Vegetable oil is more resistant to heat than animal fat is.

13

Energize Your Mind and Body with an Improved Circulation of Blood

Did you know that every cell in your body has to have food and oxygen to stay alive and healthy? Each cell also gives off waste products that must be eliminated through the lungs and kidneys. All this is taken care of by the circulation of blood—but that's only part of the story.

The blood also carries vitamins, minerals, and hormones that regulate and coordinate the action of cells and organs. Antibodies in the blood protect the cells against invasion by bacteria and other foreign substances. If germs do break through the defensive membranes of the body, the blood stream transports in an army of germ-killing white cells that literally eat the invaders alive.

Like a perpetually flowing river of life, your blood stream keeps you alive. It can also keep you healthy if it's properly nourished and stimulated. With improved circulation, your kidneys and other organs will function better. An increase flow of blood through the liver will step up your body's disposal of toxins.

The liver, which is a service station as well as a supply house, receives depleted blood and then releases it filled with fuel for your muscles and building blocks for your tissues.

YOUR HEART CAN'T DO THE JOB ALONE

A strong, healthy heart muscle will do most of the work for you in circulating your blood, but it won't do it all. Because of the static postures most of us must assume during the course of a working day, it would be helpful to make a special effort to flush certain portions of the body with a fresh flow of blood. Even the brain can benefit from an increased flow of blood several times a day.

If you carry out the simple recommendations outlined in this chapter, you can bathe your body internally with enough blood to build better health, fight off disease, improve thinking, and prolong life.

WHAT MAKES YOUR BLOOD CIRCULATE?

We all know that the heart pumps blood. So do the arteries. With each contraction of the heart muscle, the arteries expand to accommodate the sudden outflow of blood. Then, between heart beats, the recoiling elastic arteries keep pushing the blood along until another heart contraction pumps out more blood.

BLOOD PRESSURE: When your doctor takes your blood pressure, the highest figure he records is the pressure generated by each heart beat—or, more accurately, the resistance the blood meets in moving through the arteries. Death occurs when the heart stops beating and the blood pressure drops to zero.

As long as the heart is functioning, however, there are other factors that play important roles in the circulation of blood. Once you know what these are and how they work, you can do a great deal to help your heart circulate a maximum amount of blood.

HOW GRAVITY AFFECTS YOUR BLOOD CIRCULATION

If we walked on four legs as most animals do, gravity wouldn't be such a factor in the circulation of blood. But as two-legged animals walking in an upright posture, we humans must make special adaptations to the forces of gravity if we are to supply our brain, as well as our feet, with adequate blood.

Whenever we sit or stand, the circulation of arterial blood below the heart is aided by gravity, while that above the heart is hindered by gravity.

When the blood reaches the veins, however, the effect of gravity is reversed. For example, the return of venous blood above the heart is aided by gravity, whereas the uphill flow of venous blood below the heart is hindered by gravity.

If it were not for the effect that breathing and exercise have on the venous flow below the heart, the flow of blood might not be able to complete its circuit through the body when we stand erect.

Arterial and venous blood can circulate freely when we are lying down, but few of us can do a day's work in a supine position.

Fortunately, the human body has pretty much adapted to the interference of gravity by using its lungs and its muscles to aid in the pumping of blood. Some four-legged animals, on the other hand, will die if suspended in an upright position for very long. A rabbit, for example, will quickly faint if held up by his ears.

HOW EXERCISE HELPS YOUR BLOOD CIRCULATE

Whenever you walk or move about, the contraction of muscles squeezes the veins that weave through the muscle fibers. Since veins have one-way valves that permit the blood to flow only toward the heart, *muscular contraction actually pushes venous blood back to the heart where it can be pumped through the lungs for a new supply of oxygen.*

Each time a muscle relaxes following a contraction, its veins again fill with blood, filling and emptying like a great sponge being squeezed and released by the hand of a giant.

Soldiers, choir singers, and other persons who must stand for hours at a time without leg movement sometimes faint from a pooling of blood in their legs and abdomen. Without the rhythmical contraction of thigh muscles, the heart does not receive enough venous blood to keep up an adequate flow of arterial blood to the brain.

HOW RESPIRATION AIDS CIRCULATION

After the venous blood is pushed up through the legs and thighs by contracting muscles, it reaches the great thoracic and abdominal veins that lead directly to the heart. Each time you take a breath, the negative pressure created in the chest cavity by the expanding rib cage draws the blood up toward your heart. At the same time, the downward movement of the diaphragm compresses the lower abdomen to give the column of blood a push from the bottom.

Thus, *your diaphragm acts as an antigravity pump that gives the blood a final push near the end of its journey.* You should strengthen this important muscle by doing the breathing exercises described in Chapter 14.

How Poor Posture Can Interfere with the Respiratory Pump

Whenever you stand in a slumped position with your chest flattened and your abdomen protruding, the movement of the diaphragm is greatly limited. Instead of making a long, sweeping up and down excursion, it moves only a few inches with short, rapid respiration. This greatly interferes with the aid to circulation offered by breathing, and it allows a build-up of abdominal pressure to obstruct the circulation of blood through the liver and other important abdominal organs.

Worst of all, the compression of poor posture can place such a strain on the function of the heart that it can cause heart failure! This type of heart trouble can be corrected only by improving body mechanics. High blood pressure may also be lowered by removing postural kinks in veins and arteries.

HOW TO IMPROVE YOUR MIND POWER WITH
A SLANT BOARD

If you do much mental work, your brain needs a lot of blood to function efficiently. You already know that in a sitting or standing position the flow of blood to your brain is hindered by the pull of gravity. Obviously, the best way to give your brain a blood bath is to lie down with your head lower than your feet. This can be accomplished easily and conveniently with a slant board.

How an Executive Refreshes His Mind

A bank executive who consistently lost his ability to concentrate after several hours of work found that he could restore his mental capacity by lying down on a slant board with his feet anchored under a strap at the high end of the board.

"When I lie down on that board for a few minutes," he said, "my fatigue disappears and the cobwebs are washed right out of my brain. Now I know why those Yoga people are always standing on their head."

How a Mother Relieves Her "Female Troubles" with a Slant Board

A 31-year-old mother complaining of pelvic trouble and painful menstruation was able to relieve her symptoms by lying on a slant board for several minutes two or three times each day. The upside down posture restored circulation by removing the pressure that fallen abdominal organs were placing on her pelvic organs. Kinks were also removed from a tilted womb.

How to Make Your Own Slant Board

You can purchase a professional-looking slant board at any sporting goods store for use at home or in one corner of your office—or you can make your own board if you like.

Any kind of smoothly finished board about seven feet long, 15 inches wide, and one inch thick will do fine. You can nail a strap or an old belt around one end for anchoring your feet. For additional comfort, you might want to pad the board with a layer of cotton covered by a sheet of plastic.

How to Use Your Slant Board

Prop the strapped end of the board up on a chair and lie down on it with your head down and your feet up. The strap should anchor your feet securely so that you can lie completely relaxed. Stagnant venous blood will drain out of your lower body, and a flood of oxygen-rich arterial blood will flow downhill to your brain. (See Figure 13-1.)

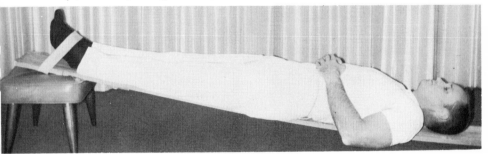

Figure 13-1. Resting on a slant board will relieve fatigue, aches, and pains by reversing the effect that gravity has on the body.

Several minutes of rest on a slant board will also relieve compression on your spine and relax your muscles with a slight traction effect. Abdominal organs will fall back into place and your heart will pump more easily. Many of the aches and pains in your muscles and joints will be relieved by reversing the pull of gravity.

HOW OVEREATING DEPRIVES YOUR BRAIN OF BLOOD

Just about everyone feels sleepy, drowsy, and unable to concentrate after eating a big meal. The reason for this is that such a large amount of blood is diverted to the digestive process that a diminished flow of blood to the brain deprives the mental processes of adequate oxygen. It takes a lot of blood to digest a big meal. There just isn't enough to supply an overload in the brain and the stomach at the same time. Even a baby's feet will feel cold from a decrease in circulation after he has eaten.

Eat lightly whenever you have some important brainwork to do. You can't empty an overloaded stomach by lying on a slant board.

HOW TO ACTIVATE THE "BLOOD PUMPS" IN YOUR LEGS AND YOUR TRUNK

If you do a lot of sitting or standing during the day, you may not use your leg muscles enough to offer your heart much aid in the circulation of blood. As a result, you may become drowsy and sleepy during working hours, or you may finish each day with a weakness that compels you to flop out on the couch just as soon as you get home. You might also suffer from swollen ankles, leg ache, cold feet, varicose veins, and other disorders caused by poor circulation through your feet and legs.

Figure 13-2. Flexing and extending the leg in a thigh-pumping exercise will pump stale blood out of the legs.

Activating the "blood pumps" in your legs, abdomen, and chest will help relieve these problems, and an increase in overall body circulation will give you new strength and energy.

A.   THIGH PUMP: Lie on your back on a rug. Bend your knees so that the soles of your feet rest flat on the floor. Then lift one leg and lock it out straight at about a 45 degree angle. Return the foot to starting position and pause about three seconds before performing another repetition. Exercise each leg equally for several repetitions. (See Figure 13-2.)

B.   TRUNK PUMP: While still lying on your back, lift both bent knees so that you can grasp them with your hands. Then, with a rocking motion, pull your knees to your chest several times, each time curling your buttocks up from the floor. Be sure to leave your glottis (throat) open so that you can exhale during each repetition. (See Figure 13-3.)

Figure 13-3. Flexing the knees on the chest while exhaling will pump blood through the trunk with a piston-like action.

This exercise will rejuvenate your abdominal organs by pumping blood through your liver.

C.   CHEST PUMP: Next, with your knees bent and your feet again flat on the floor, take a deep breath while pressing your abdomen down and upward with your hands. Do the exercise about four times, lifting your chest as high as you can each time you inhale. (See Figure 13-4.)

If this exercise makes you a little dizzy, remain lying on the floor for a few minutes before getting back on your feet.

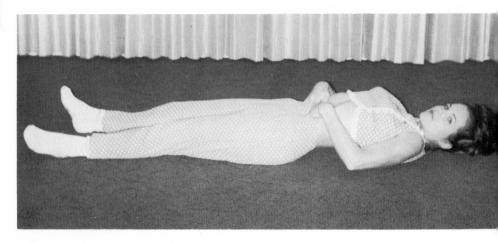

Figure 13-4. *Lifting the chest while pressing on the abdomen will improve circulation through the abdominal organs.*

LEG PAIN CAUSED BY POOR CIRCULATION

Because of the distance of the legs from the heart and the effect of gravity on the venous circulation, vascular disturbance is usually first evident in the legs. Many elderly persons who have hardened arteries, for example, complain of leg ache when they walk or stand.

A Case History of Leg Pain

A 68-year-old judge complained of pain in his calves when he walked more than a few yards. "I can walk about a block," he said, "and then my legs start aching. After I sit down for awhile, I can walk another block before they start aching again."

X-ray examination of his legs revealed that the arteries traveling down the back of his knees and calves were so hard and calcified that they could be clearly seen. He was suffering from arteriosclerosis; and whenever he used his calf muscles, they simply ached from poor circulation and lack of oxygen. Doctors call this "intermittent claudication."

I advised the judge to walk as much as he could each day but to stop and rest whenever his legs began to ache. By walking slowly and avoiding hills, he could walk a couple of blocks without too much trouble. Each day, he immersed his feet and legs first in hot water and then in cold water, as recommended in Chapter 10 (under "Contrast Bathing") for improved circulation. He also practiced the blood-pumping exercises described in this chapter.

All of this together improved the circulation of blood through his calves by opening new capillaries to form a collateral or "extra" circulation. Also, the training effect of the regular walking exercise increased the endurance of the calf muscles so that they could neutralize the waste products of muscular contraction more rapidly.

Preventing Leg Pain Caused by Poor Circulation

You can use the judge's routine to *prevent* leg pain caused by poor circulation. Chapter 5 tells you everything you need to know to prevent a build-up of fat in the walls of your arteries. The sooner you begin to observe all these rules, the better. If you're fortunate enough to begin at a youthful age, you'll have a better chance of making life's long journey with no trouble at all.

HOW TO STIMULATE OVERALL BODY CIRCULATION WITH WATER

In addition to stimulating circulation, this self-help technique will improve skin tone. A young lady who used it occasionally following her regular bath reported that her skin took on the "loving glow" of a baby.

The Salt and Water Glow

Soak in a tub of hot water for several minutes. Then drain the water from the tub and rub your body with a coarse salt that has been wet with cold water. Stop the rubbing when your skin begins to take on a pink glow. Follow this with a warm shower that's gradually turned down to a comfortably cold temperature. Dry your body with a coarse turkish towel.

The hot water and the salt will draw a maximum amount of blood to the skin. The abrasive effect of the salt will also "sand" rough areas from the surface of the skin and remove dead tissue. The cold shower will then close the pores and drive the blood inward for a vigorous circulatory stimulant.

When the circulation of blood readjusts itself to room temperature, your skin will be radiant and velvety to touch.

THE CORN MEAL BATH: If a salt rub seems to "burn" your skin, try using corn meal. First wet your body and then rub the coarse meal over your skin. Keep rubbing until the meal disappears.

Use about a tablespoonful of wet meal on each body part. When you've covered your entire body, soak in a tub of warm water before finishing up with a cold shower.

Why You Should Avoid Prolonged Exposure to Hot or Cold Water

Brief exposure to hot or cold water will increase heart rate, respiration, and circulation to stimulate the body's healing and recuperative powers. It will even increase the number of germ-killing white cells in the blood stream. Too long an exposure, however, will lower resistance by producing fatigue or by depressing body functions.

For tonic or stimulating purposes, exposure to water of extreme temperature should probably not last longer than a minute or two when the entire body is involved.

Whenever your muscles have been fatigued by exercise, a warm shower gradually reduced to cold will speed your recovery by driving the blood deep into the muscles where it's needed most.

AIDING YOUR CIRCULATION WITH MASSAGE

When you are tired from overwork and you don't feel like exercising, you can stimulate the circulation of blood through sore muscles with light massage.

Technique of Body Massage

Apply baby oil, olive oil, coco butter, cold cream, or some other type of oil to the muscles you want to massage. If you are a man and your body is hairy, coco butter will be the best lubricant.

Mineral oil mixed with alcohol is a good massage lubricant for smooth, hairless skins. The alcohol will evaporate, leaving just enough oil on the skin to prevent excessive friction. Too much oil hinders good massage technique.

Alcohol may be used to remove oil from the body when the massage is

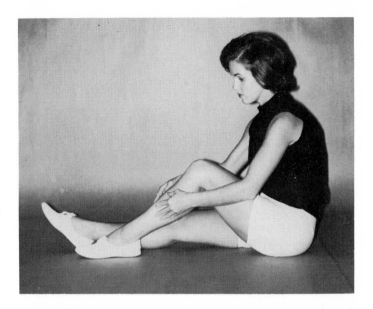

Figure 13-5. Use your fingertips when massaging your legs—and always massage toward your heart.

completed. Persons who have dry skin, however, should simply wipe the body clean with a dry rag so that a small amount of oil will remain on the skin to prevent chapping and cracking.

Always massage toward your heart so that you will push the venous blood in the right direction.

WARNING: Do not massage your legs if you have diabetes or phlebitis (inflammation of veins). Diseased or infected skin should never be massaged without doctor's orders.

Moving Gravity-Hindered Circulation Through Arms and Legs

Since the circulation of blood through the arms and legs is slowed by gravity, you can aid overall circulation by using a special massage technique over these parts of your body.

BEGIN WITH A LEG: Start with the ankle on one leg and knead the muscles in light overlapping strokes until you reach the hip. You may either grip the muscles with both hands or use your fingertips in a stroking manner. (See Figure 13-5.)

You will, of course, have to sit down and bend the knee of the leg you're massaging. Massage each leg twice and then lie down for a few minutes with your legs elevated.

END WITH AN ARM: Let your arm lie relaxed on a table top. Massage it from wrist to shoulder in one long stroke. Mold your cupped hand to the contour of your arm. Massage both arms with three or four strokes. (See Figure 13-6.)

Figure 13-6. The muscles of the arm must be completely relaxed for arm massage to be effective.

SPECIAL CARE FOR VARICOSE VEINS

If you have varicose veins, you should *elevate your legs several times a day to drain the swollen vessels.* This may be done easily and conveniently by lying on a slant board or by resting your feet on a chair or against a wall. (See Figure 13-7.) The "thigh pump" exercise described under Exercise "A" of this chapter will combine exercise and elevation for an effective way to reduce swelling.

Figure 13-7. Persons who have varicose veins should rest their feet on a wall several times a day.

Women may wear elastic hose between elevations to keep the veins from distending excessively.

Any kind of walking exercise, if done for a short period of time preceding elevation of the legs, helps to keep the blood circulating. Prolonged standing should be avoided, however. Whenever you stand, without the benefit of the pumping action of muscular contraction, the pressure in leg veins is five times greater than when you lie down. This would force a considerable amount of blood to back up through weak or defective valves in the large surface veins.

HOW TO CARE FOR HEMORRHOIDS

Since rectal hemorrhoids or "piles" are simply varicose veins, lying down on a steeply inclined slant board will help drain the accumulated blood.

Protruding internal hemorrhoids may be reduced or pressed back if a cold application is applied to the swollen veins after lying on the slant board. See your doctor if any of the veins become hard and painful.

In the case of external hemorrhoids, symptoms can be relieved better by sitting in a tub of hot water.

HEART PAIN CAUSED BY POOR CIRCULATION

If you have heart trouble, you should be under the care of a doctor. But if you have "angina pectoris," or chest pain that occurs only during exertion because of a poor blood supply to the heart muscle, you might be able to help yourself by exercising your heart lightly and progressively.

Exercise Opens Blood Vessels

The right kind of exercise will improve the heart's blood supply by widening the coronary arteries and opening new capillaries inside the heart muscle.

Begin by walking. Walk slowly at first, and stop whenever you begin to feel any pain or discomfort in your chest. As the weeks and months pass, you should be able to walk faster and farther before experiencing any pain.

When walking no longer seems to bother you, you can begin a light and progressive jogging program (see Chapter 6). As the circulation to the heart muscle improves, you can indulge in more strenuous, recreational forms of exercise, such as tennis.

SMOKING IS HARD ON YOUR ARTERIES

Remember that if you have any kind of trouble with your blood vessels or your heart, you shouldn't smoke. *The nicotine in tobacco smoke constricts blood vessels to interfere with the circulation of blood.*

THE IMPORTANCE OF A LEAN ABDOMEN

If your abdomen is sagging and you have a "pot belly," you should start doing sit-ups in a daily exercise program (see Chapter 11). Whenever the abdominal muscles stretch and sag so far that the abdominal organs are no longer held in their proper positions, they become heavy and congested from an interference in the circulation of blood. Circulation throughout the entire body is also impaired.

Practice pulling your abdomen in (see Chapter 14). Try to develop the habit of keeping your abdomen flat by keeping a little tension on your abdominal muscles.

SUMMARY

1. The circulation of blood carries food, oxygen, vitamins, minerals, hormones, antibodies, germ killers, and other substances your body needs to sustain life. It also transports waste products to the lungs and the kidneys for elimination.

2. Since gravity interferes with the circulation of venous blood when we sit and stand, the body must enlist the aid of respiration and muscular contraction in returning blood to the heart.

3. The blood-pumping exercises described in this chapter will aid the circulation of blood to flush stagnant areas and energize your body.

4. Lying down on a slant board with your head down and your feet up will relieve aches and pains in your muscles and joints and clear your brain with a fresh flow of arterial blood.

5. Walking or jogging is a good way to increase the flow of blood through your body and your heart.

6. A warm bath and a salt rub followed by a warm shower that's gradually turned down to cold is a good circulatory stimulant—and it'll give your skin a healthy glow.

7. Whenever you use massage to stimulate the circulation of blood, always massage *toward* your heart.

8. If you have varicose veins, elevate your legs several times a day to permit drainage by gravity.

9. Maintain the muscular support around your abdomen by doing regular sit-up exercises. A sagging abdomen can obstruct the flow of blood to important organs and impair the circulation of blood throughout the body.

10. Smoking interferes with the circulation of blood by constricting tiny arteries.

Breathe New Life into Your Body

Most of us take our breathing for granted— until something happens to interfere with this vital process. Anyone suffering from asthma, emphysema, and other diseases of the lungs can tell you that normal, natural breathing is a *priceless* treasure.

Take a deep breath. Feel your lungs expand with the wonderfully refreshing air that gives you life. Just imagine how miserable and how anxious you would be if you couldn't expand your lungs fully or if you couldn't quite get enough air.

Breathing is essential. It can also be a pleasure. But if you don't cultivate good breathing habits and then seek clean, fresh air, you'll short-change your health as well as your comfort. If you allow this to happen, you may wake up one day and discover that a phantom hand is squeezing your lungs.

BATHING YOUR BLOOD WITH AIR

After the circulation of blood has completed its circuit through the body, it must be pumped through the lungs where carbon dioxide is exchanged for life-giving oxygen. Without oxygen, the chemical processes that make life possible could not take place. The brain and the heart, in particular, must have a consistently rich supply of oxygen in order to function efficiently.

A RIGHT WAY AND A WRONG WAY TO BREATHE

Fortunately, breathing is, for the most part, an unconscious and automatic process, so you don't have to worry about getting enough oxygen when you drop off to sleep. But when you are awake and active, there is a right way and a wrong way to breathe. You must, in fact breathe correctly or suffer from certain disturbing side effects.

Most of us don't breathe enough, while some of us breathe too much. Very few people know enough about the mechanics of breathing to voluntarily aid respiration in the best possible way.

This chapter will tell you how to breathe new life into your body by using the muscles of your chest and abdomen in a special way. There are also ways to tell when your body is making a balanced and efficient exchange of carbon dioxide for oxygen.

If you can learn to use your lungs fully and properly in correct breathing techniques, you can improve the function of every cell and organ in your body. You can, in fact, literally bathe your body internally with a sea of cleansing air.

THE DANGERS OF SHALLOW BREATHING

If you're one of the millions of Americans who lead a sedentary life, you have probably developed the habit of shallow breathing; that is, you may be using only the top portion of your lungs in frequent, short breaths. This means that a large portion of your lungs is always filled with stale, dead air that blocks absorption of oxygen and the elimination of carbon dioxide.

An inadequate supply of oxygen to the brain can cause mental confusion and drowsiness. In addition, a backing up of carbon dioxide in muscles, organs, and other tissues may clog your body's machinery to create physical fatigue or illness.

THE EFFECTS OF OXYGEN STARVATION

Under some circumstances, especially while you are at rest, you may not know that you're not getting enough oxygen if you're able to inhale and exhale without any trouble. Pilots, for example, who fly at high altitudes without an artificial oxygen supply, may not realize that they're suffering from oxygen deficiency, even though their behavior may be very erratic.

The Car as a Gas Chamber

Every winter, a number of people die from breathing stale air in closed automobiles. The victims are usually travelers who stop by the road to sleep, lovers who park in a "lover's lane," and others trying to keep warm by closing all the windows and leaving the car engine running for heat. These people go to sleep—and die—without ever realizing that exhaust fumes are depriving them of oxygen.

Make sure that the muffler on your car doesn't leak. If it does, don't close all the windows of your car while its engine is running.

It's not very likely that you'll die from lack of oxygen where you work and live. But you may not be getting *enough* oxygen, and you may not be aware of the deficiency.

"Bad Air" Where You Work

Poorly ventilated buildings that contain excessive amounts of carbon dioxide from the lungs of workers, or too much carbon monoxide from the exhaust of machines or heaters, may deprive you of adequate oxygen. This can make your day long and miserable—until you can step outside for "a breath of fresh air."

The Case of the Oxygen-Starved Bookkeeper

A normally energetic bookkeeper who worked in a small office in one corner of a large garage couldn't understand why her "nerves" were so bad or why she suffered from headache and exhaustion at the end of each day.

"Sometimes I get so confused I could scream," lamented Sally J. "And I just cannot concentrate on my book work. My doctor says that there is nothing organically wrong with me."

Sally J. was suffering from carbon monoxide poisoning and lack of fresh air. When her employer installed heating and cooling units that circulated air from the outside, she recovered her energy and alertness and she no longer had any trouble keeping her books.

WARNING: Don't work or play in areas where the air is filled with exhaust fumes. The hemoglobin in your red blood cells will absorb the carbon monoxide from these fumes about 200 times more readily than it will absorb oxygen. Once carbon monoxide gets into your blood, it stays there for many hours and tends to prevent the release of oxygen to your tissues. This can cause a variety of bizarre symptoms from both carbon monoxide poisoning and oxygen starvation.

Make sure that the air you breathe is fresh and clean. If there is not an unhindered exchange of carbon dioxide for oxygen in your lungs, the cells of your body won't be able to "breathe," and an accumulation of waste products will interfere with the processes of life.

OZONE: NATURE'S AIR TONIC

Everyone has had the experience of leaving a stuffy classroom or theater to be revived by cool currents of outdoor air. Night air that has been cooled by darkness and filtered by moisture provides us with pure breathing pleasure.

Falling rain drops or a heavy dew or fog literally washes the air clean of dust, smoke, germs, and other debris, leaving it charged with a stimulating form of oxygen called "ozone."

Air saturated and agitated by the mist of a waterfall or the breakers of a seashore is especially clean and stimulating. The oxygen-rich, high ozone content of such water-washed air will perk you up better than any tonic you'll every swallow.

THE DANGERS OF OVERBREATHING

Since we use only about one-fourth of our lung space during ordinary breathing, it's necessary for us to occasionally breathe deeply in order to clean out our lungs and to keep the air sacs expanded and flexible. Unless exercise has created a need for oxygen, however, you shouldn't breathe too deeply too often. Overbreathing has many side effects, some of which can be serious.

What Happens When You Overbreathe?

Ordinarily, the rate and depth of your breathing will be governed by the amount of oxygen your muscles need and the amount of carbon dioxide released by muscular contraction. Whenever the carbon dioxide content of the blood is raised above a certain level, it stimulates the respiratory centers of the brain to step up the action of the lungs.

Even when you are completely rested, a certain amount of carbon dioxide in your blood maintains breathing and dilates the blood vessels around your brain for better utilization of oxygen.

When you overbreathe or hyperventilate, your lungs siphon too much carbon dioxide out of your blood. This constricts the blood vessels around your brain and upsets the carbon dioxide–oxygen balance in your blood to cause dizziness and other symptoms. It may even cause blackout if forced breathing is continued after the dizziness begins.

Many persons have "keeled over" unconscious after taking breathing exercises that have not been preceded by physical exercise.

An Example of Blackout Caused by Overbreathing

A minister who fell and injured himself when he blacked out in his bathroom did not associate his deep breathing exercises with the incident until it happened a second time. When he learned that hyperventilation not preceded by exercise could *decrease* the oxygen supply to his brain rather than increase it, he elected to do his breathing exercises after jogging rather than after brushing his teeth.

A BREATHING RULE: While you should breathe deeply many times during the day, you shouldn't take more than two or three deep breaths at one time when you are rested. Always discontinue deep breathing when you begin to feel a little dizzy or light headed.

OVERBREATHING CAUSED BY ANXIETY

If you suffer from anxiety or nervousness, you may be overbreathing without realizing it. If so, you might eventually suffer from vertigo, impaired vision, irregular heart beat, numbness, tingling, and other symptoms caused by a chronic imbalance of the oxygen and carbon dioxide content of your blood. In many cases, such symptoms will defy diagnosis.

If you or your doctor fails to recognize your tendency to hyperventilate when you get nervous, you may be subjected to all kinds of medical examinations in a search for organic disease.

The Case of Lucy C.

Mrs. Lucy C., a 64-year-old widow, complained of shortness of breath, heart palpitation, and dizziness. "I just can't get my breath," she complained, "and I get so dizzy that I have to lie down several times a day." Her family physician assured her that her heart was normal and that he could find no organic basis for her trouble.

When I talked to Mrs. C., I noticed that she was extremely nervous and that she was constantly sighing. The more nervous she became, the more she sighed—until she began to gasp for breath with the desperation of an asthmatic. It soon became apparent that her real trouble was anxiety, and that some dark, terrible thought was probably triggering her respiration until hyperventilation created disturbing side effects.

I told Lucy C. that she should try to resolve her emotional problems and then make a special effort to quit sighing or overbreathing. The next time I saw her, she told me that she no longer had trouble with her breath and that her dizziness and other symptoms had disappeared. Just learning that her trouble was emotional rather than organic was enough to relieve her anxiety.

RELIEVING HYPERVENTILATION WITH A PAPER BAG

If you suffer from sighing or hyperventilation that you find difficult to control, try this little trick. Fit a six-pound paper bag snugly over your nose and mouth and breathe into it for a few minutes or until your breathing is back to normal—never longer than five minutes. Remove the bag if you begin to experience any unusual symptoms. (See Figure 14-1.)

Breathing into the bag will restore the carbon dioxide your body needs to control respiration and blood circulation, and it will relieve uncomfortable sighing. Actors, politicians, businessmen, and other persons who suffer from anxiety caused by social pressures, business engagements, speeches, public appearances, and other nerve-racking responsibilities have been advised to use a paper bag to ease the breathlessness that leads to hyperventilation just before "meeting the public."

You can do the same. Just fold up a bag and put it in your back pocket or your handbag. Then, when you are confronted by something or someone who makes you nervous, just put the bag over your mouth and nose and take two or three—or several—deep breaths. The high CO_2 (carbon dioxide) content of the bag will prevent excessive exchange of carbon dioxide for oxygen. Remember that "nervous breathing" is triggered by nerves rather than by a need for oxygen.

A HICCUP BONUS: The next time you have hiccups, try breathing into your paper bag. This has been found to be an effective way to control this aggravating, but not usually serious, diaphragmatic disturbance.

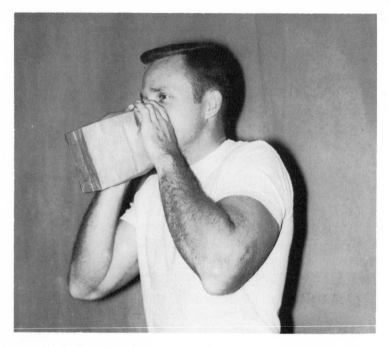

Figure 14-1. *Breathing into a paper bag will relieve dizziness and other symptoms caused by nervous overbreathing.*

HYPERVENTILATION AS A CAUSE OF ANXIETY

Some persons who develop the habit of overbreathing suffer from anxiety not because of emotional problems but because of the symptoms of hyperventilation. Mr. Charles D., for example, who practiced deep breathing as a health practice, tried to relieve his symptoms with even more deep breathing. When his dizziness and mental confusion grew worse instead of better, his anxiety turned to panic and he visited a large medical clinic for a checkup.

"I thought I was seriously ill," he confessed, "until I found out that I was just overbreathing. When I quit trying to breathe away my symptoms, my symptoms disappeared."

The examples of Lucy C. and Charles D. aren't intended to discourage you from breathing deeply. Quite the contrary. You should breathe deeply many times during the day, but not to the point of overbreathing.

If you want to practice forced deep breathing for a long period of time, or for more than two or three breaths at a time, you should first create an oxygen "debt" by exercising so that your breathing will *restore* the proper balance of oxygen and carbon dioxide rather than upset it.

HOW TO BREATHE CORRECTLY

Whenever you're rested and breathing quietly, your breathing is naturally abdominal; that is, there is more movement in your abdomen than in your chest. Your chest muscles remain relaxed while your abdomen rises and falls. The abdominal muscles are relaxed, however, while the involuntary up and down movement of the diaphragm pumps a small amount of air in and out of the upper portion of the lungs.

When exercise or exertion compels you to breathe deeply, your diaphragm moves down as before, but certain chest muscles aid respiration by expanding the rib cage to permit a greater intake of air.

Abdominal Breathing versus Thoracic Breathing

Some persons try to distinguish thoracic breathing from abdominal breathing, saying that one is good and the other bad. Actually, the type of breathing you do depends largely upon the amount of oxygen you need—except, of course, when you're taking special breathing exercises.

The Importance of Abdominal Breathing

In the course of the ordinary day, you should breathe in a way that is most natural to you. That is, you should not have to concentrate on breathing or make a special effort to breathe in a certain way. Several times each day, however, you should breathe deeply into your abdomen, letting your stomach bulge out as far as it will go. This will assure expansion of the lower lobes of your lungs. And in order to make sure that you get enough fresh air in your lungs to dilute the stale air in the far corners of your lungs, you should *exhale* as much air as you can before taking a deep breath.

Persons who breathe shallowly use less than one-quarter of their total lung space. This allows the rest of the lungs to fill with carbon dioxide. Even with a maximum exhalation, a certain amount of stale air remains in the lungs. A long, deep breath of fresh air, however, will mix enough "new" air with "old" air to freshen all of the lobes and sacs of the lungs.

Do not take more than two or three deep breaths in succession. Remember what you learned about hyperventilation.

BREATHING AND GOOD POSTURE

As a rule, abdominal breathing should be done while you're relaxed and unobserved. When you're trying to maintain good posture in an erect standing position, it would be difficult to breathe into your abdomen while trying to hold your "stomach" in. Once you develop the habit of keeping a flat abdomen in maintaining good posture, you can lift your chest a little and breathe normally without thought or difficulty.

BREATHING DURING EXERCISE

Just as you automatically breathe into your abdomen when you're relaxed and rested, you'll automatically lift your chest when you breathe following exercise. With abdominal breathing alone, you cannot ventilate your lungs enough to meet your body's increased need for oxygen.

Whenever you indulge in any kind of exercise, satisfy your oxygen debt by breathing deeply, lifting your chest as high as you can. This will assure both abdominal and thoracic breathing. You know from reading Chapter 13 that such breathing also aids the circulation of blood by creating a pump-like negative pressure in the thoracic cavity.

Don't ever hold your breath while exercising. Always exhale during an exertion, especially when the abdominal muscles are being contracted.

The worst thing you can do is to hyperventilate and then take a deep breath and hold it during a prolonged exertion. The forced deep breathing will constrict the blood vessels around your brain by "blowing off" too much carbon dioxide. If this is followed by a sudden need for oxygen in contracting muscles, along with compression of the lungs in breath holding, the flow of blood to the brain will be drastically diminished. If you don't faint from oxygen deficiency around your brain, you might "blowout" an artery.

It is a fad among some teenagers to deliberately induce a blackout by taking several deep breaths in a standing position and then holding the final breath while blowing against their thumb in a squatting position. This has proved to be an extremely dangerous practice. Don't try it.

HOW TO EXERCISE YOUR BREATHING MUSCLES

You can both strengthen your breathing muscles and increase the capacity of your lungs by doing a few special breathing exercises a couple of times a week.

A coach, an insurance salesman, and a dancing instructor who took these exercises reported an improvement in endurance as well as better health and increased vitality.

"Since I started taking these breathing exercises," the dancing instructor said, "I don't get nearly as tired as I used to after dancing all day. And I sleep better at night. Even my waistline is more firm and trim."

1. Exercising Your Diaphragm with Forced Expiration

Force as much air out of your lungs as you can with a maximum expiration. Contract your abdominal muscles in the process so that your diaphragm will be forced to move far up into your chest.

You can exercise your diaphragm against resistance by exhaling vigorously through pursed lips or through a small drinking straw. Trying to blow up a balloon with as few breaths as possible is also a good exercise for the abdominal muscles and the diaphragm. (See Figure 14-2.)

Figure 14-2. Exhaling vigorously through a small drinking straw will strengthen important "breathing out" muscles.

CAUTION: Make sure that forced exhalation is unobstructed. If you attempt to breathe out without any air escaping from your lungs, a build-up of pressure in your chest and abdomen might interfere with the circulation of blood enough to cause a blackout. You might also develop an abdominal hernia (Chapter 11).

2. The Abdominal Vacuum

Stand with your knees and your back slightly bent (forward) and your hands on your thighs. Exhale, hold your breath, and then draw your stomach up into your chest by attempting to inhale up through your abdomen. Keep your glottis (throat) closed throughout the exercise. (See Figure 14-3.)

Figure 14-3. Performing a stomach vacuum will strengthen "breathing in" muscles and massage the abdominal organs.

Press against your thighs very lightly with your hands so that you can lift your chest higher for a greater suction effect. The abdominal muscles should remain relaxed so that they can follow the diaphragm up into the chest.

Do this exercise several times a day. In addition to exercising the breathing muscles that lift your chest, it will massage your abdominal organs.

3. The Isometric Chest Expander

This exercise will expand your rib cage and give you a deeper, more attractive chest. Since it forces maximum expansion of the rib cage as well as the lungs, it will be more effective if done immediately following some kind of exercise that makes you breathe heavily.

Stand erect and place your hands on a bar, a tree limb, a ledge, or some other surface about level with the bottom of your rib cage. Lock your arms out straight and then press downward a little with your hands as you inhale. This will anchor your shoulder girdle so that you can use certain chest muscles to lift your ribs higher than you could otherwise. (See Figure 14-4.)

Figure 14-4. This isometric chest-expanding exercise will expand the upper lobes of the lungs.

With each breath, lift your chest as high as you can. Your abdominal muscles should remain relaxed throughout the exercise.

Do the exercise only two or three times when you're rested. When you're breathless from taking some other form of exercise, do as many repetitions as necessary to satisfy your body's need for extra oxygen.

4. The Stomach Lift

Lie on your back on the floor. Place a ten-pound sandbag (or a similar object) on your abdomen over your navel. Then lift the weight up and down with your abdomen. Inhale as you lift the weight and then exhale as you lower it. Although you'll be using your abdominal muscles to some extent, your diaphragm will do most of the work. (See Figure 14-5.)

Figure 14-5. Lifting a light weight on the abdomen will fully activate the diaphragm and expand the lower lobes of the lungs.

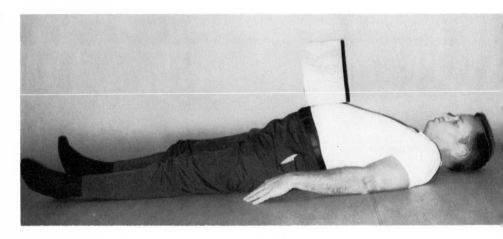

SUMMARY

1. The circulation of blood through your lungs exchanges carbon dioxide waste for life-giving oxygen.

2. Habitual shallow breathing ventilates only a portion of the upper lobes of the lungs.

3. Breathe deeply into your abdomen several times a day, but stop whenever you begin to feel a little dizzy.

4. When you are breathless from taking exercise, breathe deeply by lifting your chest. Inhale as many times as necessary to satisfy your body's need for extra oxygen.

5. Hyperventilation, or forced deep breathing, can cause headache, dizziness, and other symptoms if practiced without first exercising to create a need for oxygen in the muscles.

6. Persons who are constantly sighing or overbreathing because of nervousness or anxiety very often suffer from the symptoms of hyperventilation.

7. Symptoms caused by nervous overbreathing can be relieved by breathing into a paper bag that's fitted tightly over the mouth and nose.

8. Practice the breathing exercises described in this chapter to strengthen your "breathing muscles" and to increase the capacity of your lungs.

9. Air washed by falling rain or the mist of a waterfall is one of nature's most stimulating tonics.

Index